WHAT NOT TO WEAR TO A MURDER TRIAL

And Other Tips Tragedy Taught Me

BY

BARBARA ALLEN

WHAT NOT TO WEAR TO A MURDER TRIAL

Ordering Information: Quantity sales. Special discounts are available on quantity purchases by corporations, associations, and others. Orders by U.S. trade bookstores and wholesalers.

COVER CREDITS

Cover photo: Jennifer Lynch
Cover photo concept: Dave Brown
Cover pre-shoot: Beth McGowan

DREAMSTARTERS

www.DreamStartersPublishing.com

Table Of Contents

FOREWORD

"Riveting, yet devastating. Unimaginable, yet truly relatable. People believe that just because something horrible has never happened means it won't. But it can and it has. Barb Allen has faced the Devil himself more than once… and won. Everyone has hit 'rock bottom'. Some have given up. Barb has not. In 'What Not to Wear to a Murder Trial', Barb Allen delineates what it is like to be at your worst. To know that everything is against you. And how to rise up. Not just to survive the worst, but how to excel in the face of it. This is not just a story of how to survive, it is a true story of how to make others better while surviving."

-Robert J. O'Neill
Former SEAL Team Six Operator

"This book is the field manual for building life resiliency. Barbara lays it all out there!"

Bedros Keuilian, Founder of Fit Body Boot Camp

"Barb Allen has done it again! Do yourself a favor today and read this book!"

Tim Klund, CEO Verve Systems

"Barb lands a perfect balance between reality, humor, adversity and imperfection. She allows the reader to be human, make mistakes and come out tougher, stronger, and more resilient than before."

Anthony Russo, Founder/CEO BetheChange

"If you're looking for a book that will make you throw all your excuses out the window, this is it. Through her tragedy has come tremendous purpose for Barb Allen. She is authentic, raw and totally walks in her own truth. Barb will make you laugh, cry and give you the tools to overcome any obstacle, all while reminding you that you're never alone. This is a must read for anyone who is ready to tackle adversity head on, and start living the life they were meant to."

Rebekah Gregory, Boston Marathon Bombing Survivor, Founder of Rebekah's Angels

"This is a must read book for anyone who feels stuck, and overwhelmed by life's challenges. Barb shares her experiences in a fun and unique way that keeps you entertained while sharing valuable life lessons"

Marie Cosgrove, Author, CEO at Balanceback

"Barb nails the art of perfecting imperfection in this raw, sometimes sarcastic, and on-point guide to crushing adversity"

Taya Kyle

"This book could also easily be titled: How Not to Be a Little Bitch!"

Ray Care

"Don't wait for a reason to read this book - keep it on your list to read over and over, because it's a perfect tool to fine-tune your mindset anytime!"

Jeremy Harrell
Founder and CEO, Veteran's Club Inc

"Barb Allen is a true patriot and prolific author. She nailed it with her first book 'Front Toward Enemy' and she nails it again with this one turning a painful past into a powerful future. You're an inspiration Barb Allen!"

Max Martini

To the people who have loved me through all the versions of myself—thank you.

I am blessed to have you in my life.

To the people who have hurt me—thank you.

You forced me to learn how to rise above you.

To Trevor, Colin, Sean, and Jeremy: Thank you for being my "Little Leaders" for so many years and for being my constant reminders of all that is beautiful in life. Also, you may want to skip some parts of this book.

To Hayley and Logan: Thank you for rolling with the love your dad has for me and my boys. You two are my bonuses in this life.

To Dave: I made a lot of mistakes before I found you. I even put one in a book. Some of those mistakes were fun, and some of them were the opposite of fun. But they all led me to you. Thank you for coming back for a second kiss, for moving your life to build ours, and for standing by me through all the insanity we conquer and create together. You are my reward for not giving up on love.

"Those who can adapt to the situation are victorious."

Du You

The Art of War

Introduction

I will never forget the moment evil finally beat me. The heavy air in the packed courtroom, the battle between hope and hopelessness in my heart, the look on the face of the only juror who met my eyes— it's all burned into my brain. So, too, is the sound of the gavel hitting the desk, the words "That's it" coming from the prosecutor's mouth and, most of all, the way the defense attorney's expression snapped from surprise to true fear as he watched my face change from horror to hatred.

In that moment, as I lunged toward my husband's newly acquitted killer and the MPs stopped me, that defense attorney realized what I had just realized myself: I had lost the battle for my inner peace. I was in that moment filled with the kind of rage borne only out of complete hopelessness for anything other than a life with no meaning. I was no longer envisioning a future in which I could somehow piece my life back together. I was instead fantasizing about the satisfaction I would feel from stabbing my stiletto straight through the killer's eyeball to pierce his evil brain.

All the pain we'd endured, all the years we'd spent placing our faith in the system, all the healing we'd attached to an outcome we had no control over had been worse than if we'd done nothing at all. It had all served only to complete the task of shattering any possibility that I would ever be able to make my life matter again.

In that moment and the months after, I was trapped in the hold of hopelessness. I struggled with suicidal thoughts. I believed my kids would be better off without me. Anger, apathy, self-pity, fear, and defeat were the masters of my life. By day I took care of my kids and did what had to be done. The moments I played with my boys were the only moments I was able to occasionally glimpse a purpose and potential joy. Other than that, I truly didn't care what happened to me anymore.

If I'd only known then what I know now, I would have been able to navigate the trauma of those years so much better. I would have met the news of my husband's death from a place of strength instead of predetermined defeat. I would have been able to detach my self-prognosis

9

of happiness and hope from the outcome of a situation I could not control. I would have been a better mom. I would have never been vulnerable to the predator who undid all the healing I began to achieve and scorched the earth before I got rid of him.

But that was then.

Today I've taken my life back. I see beauty in even the worst days. I absorb, process, and overcome challenges, loss, and pain at light speed. I learn from it all and use those lessons to avoid repeating mistakes.

I am happier, healthier, more present, and more appreciative of life than I was before tragedy and trauma double-teamed me.

That doesn't mean life is perfect or that I am not still in need of improvement. It just means I understand the ebb and flow of life and how to ride it. I make it a point to work on making myself a better version of me today than I was yesterday.

I'll also never forget the moment I made the decision to take my life back. I can feel the summer sun burning my cheeks, hear the horses nickering in the paddock, and see the phone I'd just dropped lying beside where I knelt, sobbing, on my driveway.

It was my lowest moment where I'd finally punched right through rock bottom and stepped into its underworld. My ex-fiancé had just called me— collect—from the rehab center. I made the mistake of thinking he was calling to say he was sorry and wish me a happy birthday. Instead, he asked me for more money. I barely stammered out a "no" through my shock before he hung up on me.

There was no apology for the years of emotional, drug, and alcohol abuse; the times he'd pass out on the floor or fly into a blacked-out rage; or for taking tens of thousands of dollars from me, depleting all my savings, and leaving me with a negative checking account to address large debt.

Not to mention breaking my heart and shattering my four innocent children's hopes—again. He didn't wish me happy birthday either. As birthdays go, it was the worst one I'd ever had, and that includes no one coming to my sixteenth birthday.

So how did my lowest moment turn into the first moment of my comeback? How did I climb out from under the massive mountain of misery and hopelessness and start that climb up to life with a much prettier view? How can what I went through help you?

Fair questions, and I answer all of them in these pages. Fear not; I don't just count on my own experience to answer these questions for you—I pulled powerful nuggets of wisdom from some of the 200 guests I've interviewed for our American Snippets podcast. So in addition to my own thoughts and insight, you'll be learning from genuine military heroes, survivors of unspeakable trauma, entrepreneurs who've overcome defeat to build multimillion-dollar companies, and people who go above and beyond for the sake of others.

Whatever mistakes you've made, whatever humiliation you've had, whatever heartache you've endured, or whatever situation you're in, I promise there is something in this book that you can pull out and apply to your own life to begin making *this moment*, right now, better.

Not perfect—not magically fixing whatever is wrong—but helping you understand how to turn all the pain, anger, fear, and hopelessness into your allies instead of your enemies.

Let's do it.

***

How to Get the Most Out of This Book

Inspiration without action is just entertainment. If I do my job well, this book will entertain you in many places. But that's not my true intent. As much as I like providing entertainment, that's not why I wrote this book. I wrote this book for a very selfish reason: it allows me to flip the power of all my pain into a positive purpose.

Ask yourself: What's the worst that can happen if you go all-in on reading this book? If your time matters as much to you as mine does to me, then I beg you—please don't waste your time reading this if you don't truly want to use it as a tool to change the trajectory of your life.

- Decide and commit to finding at least one message that you connect directly to. Commit right now, before you read the first chapter, to being all-in when you read this book.
- Be completely honest with yourself when you absorb this book. If you recognize yourself in any part of what you read—good or bad—highlight it and stop to acknowledge it for a moment.
- Do the things you will be prompted to do. Do them right then and there, as you are reading, to avoid finding excuses not to do them later.

Chapter One
Mindset Matters

"Don't be a hero," I told my husband. "Don't put your life at risk to save someone else. That's not your decision to make. You don't have a right to make that choice for your wife and your children." Really. Those words literally came out of my mouth—and I was just getting started.

"If you die, I have no interest in a life without you. I could never do this on my own."

I could go on, but you get the point.

Not only did I place that weight on Lou's shoulders, but I also set myself up to maximize the carnage in my world and our children's worlds in the event that something *did* happen to Lou.

Months before my doorbell rang to confirm the gut feeling I already had, I had ensured I would suffer and languish in pain and destruction far more than I needed to.

Before my husband set foot in Iraq, I had decided that I would only be okay if he returned home to us.

It's a common practice, I know. We often tell ourselves the following:

Everything will be great as long as this happens, or that happens. We convince ourselves that *if only* we get that job or that promotion or that boyfriend, or *if only* we win that game or get that house or whatever else it is we are pinning our happiness on happens, we will be fine.

What happens then? Either that thing happens and we feel temporary happiness, or it does not happen and we stew in stress or misery because we'd convinced ourselves that we needed a different outcome. We programmed our minds and our emotions to crash instead of preparing both to recover from a shock or a sting.

Why do we do that to ourselves?

You know, honestly, I began my own self-sabotage years before Lou died. Two years of relentless and vicious harassment from four classmates, from sixth grade through eighth grade, molded me into a person with no self-confidence. I'd been suicidal in seventh grade. I'd struggled awkwardly through high school and college, and by the time I met Lou I'd almost given up on knowing what it was like to be loved.

So when he turned those hazel eyes onto mine and cracked that grin of his, I went completely under. I kid you not, there was not one day in the eleven years we had together that I did not feed the mindset that I was only *anything* because of him.

Lou had this energy and this wisdom about him that made it so even if he annoyed me he'd make me laugh a minute later, which only annoyed me more. The number of times he lost patience with my insecurity and tears were far less than they could have been.

I was completely dependent upon him for my happiness and very, very blessed that he chose to love me.

Not that there's anything wrong with loving someone so much; it's just that placing the responsibility for our own happiness on someone else's shoulders is an injustice to ourselves and that person. It also ensures we will struggle much harder when we lose that person.

The same is true for any goal we set. For me, after Lou was killed, that goal became revenge.

I lived to see his killer die.

Taking care of my boys and seeing Lou's killer die became the only things that mattered to me. I invested every ounce of myself into both of those things. Everything else seemed inconsequential.

So when I watched Lou's killer walk out of court as a free man three-and-a-half years later, I was totally unprepared to withstand the blow.

I came completely undone.

To further complicate things, I'd entered into a relationship that was the opposite of good for me. It was a relationship that never would have happened had other events not led to me feeling completely, totally alone. I felt half the people I counted on betrayed and hurt me, and the other half could simply not even come close to understanding my pain. He entered the picture just in time to "save me."

I was weak. I was broken. I was afraid, and I was exhausted. I moved into the house next door to him and slowly he became a friend. Then he became a confidant. Then he became my only ally who knew everything happening behind the scenes in my life. He was the only one who saw the cruelty of people who judged me, and the only one who saw me sobbing at night when the kids went to bed.

He would put his arms around me and tell me the lies I needed to hear: "It's okay. I will protect you."

I mean, all I wanted was to be protected from the pain. All I wished for was to make it stop. It was overwhelming, and it was everywhere.

It was in the eyes of my one son, who rarely smiled anymore. It was in the questions my kids asked about their dad, and the army, and what was going to happen now. I couldn't answer those questions and I couldn't bring the sincerity back to their smiles.

I was all alone trying to raise four little boys while the pain gripped me harder and harder and would not let go.

I did find the strength to end that relationship, however clumsily. It was a drawn-out process that maximized the pain for my boys as well, who did not understand why he'd come into our lives in the first place, or why he was leaving now.

Many people judged me for getting into the relationship, and again for getting out.

It was a lose-lose situation, as far as I saw it.

So I figured I may as well have a party.

"Barb's Bash" didn't fix any of my problems. But it did distract me from them for a few days.

Friends flew in from around the country—other military widows fleeing their own pain and doing their best to support me through mine. Close to sixty people showed up. There was an apocalyptic storm that day, causing flight delays, downed trees, blinding rain, and deadly lightning. The wind whipped around, and the rain drenched us to the core.

It was amazing.

I rented a mechanical bull for the occasion. We cleaned out a shed and set it up in there and some of us had bruises that lasted for weeks.

The storm subsided late at night. We assembled under the tent; I broke out the last few bottles of wine from the case Lou gave me on his last day home, and we toasted together.

It was easy to pretend that that moment signified a change for me. It was easy to believe, for a little while, that the worst was behind me and all I had to do now was move away from the pain, into a new life.

But because nothing had truly changed inside of me, I was in for a whole lot more pain where that had come from. And this time it brought friends, bossy ones who ruled me for years.

Much of this could have been avoided if I'd greeted tragedy with an entirely different mindset.

Lou had tried to instill confidence in me. If I'd accepted those lessons, I would have been far better off. Instead, I'd gotten mad at him.

He'd straight-up told me one day, as we talked about a widowed aunt of his, that he would remarry if something ever happened to me. He'd told me I should do the same.

His logic was that we were both young and life was much better when spent with someone you love. He wouldn't want me to be alone. He'd want me to love again and by the same token, he wouldn't want to spend his life alone either. There would be nothing we could do about the other one being dead, so the one remaining may as well live the happiest life they could.

That conversation took place about two years before he died, which is almost as long as it took for me to stop being mad at him for saying he could ever love someone else. *That's* what I took from his remarkably insightful comments—jealousy. I even told him if I died young, and he loved someone after me, *I'd come back and haunt him.*

Quite the gem, wasn't I?

Imagine for a moment if I'd had a different mindset when that conversation took place, or the one right before he left. Imagine if I'd understood the gift he'd been giving me at that moment, and the gift I could have given both of us in either moment.

Imagine if I'd agreed with him the first time and assured him that I, too, would want him to be happy, that I wouldn't want him to be lonely for the rest of his life out of loyalty to me. That I would want him to love again, and to be loved, as well. Imagine what that would have meant to him, how that would have planted a seed of resilience and hope in my heart that could have blossomed when I needed it to.

Imagine if, instead of telling Lou that he did not have the right to make me a widow and his children fatherless, I'd said instead that I loved him, and wanted nothing more than for him to come home, but that I would be proud of him no matter what, and would understand that he wanted to come home, too. If I'd told him that I would take good care of our children, and he didn't have to worry about us—that he could be free to focus on the task at hand instead.

Imagine what that could have done for him. Imagine if, as he lay wounded and became aware that he was about to die, he could have had the comfort of that conversation, of me telling him we'd love him forever and I would be okay, that our children would be okay too.

Imagine if I'd had the same seed begin to bloom in my mind—the seed of strength and grace and resilience. Imagine if I'd been able to surrender to the pain with the mindset that, as difficult as it would be, I would one day rise from it.

Do you think I'd have given up the way I did, when the trail twisted and turned, or when people hurt me?

I don't.

Do you think I'd have moved into another seven years of increasingly terrible times if I'd reached out for help instead of pretending that I didn't need it?

Probably not.

Mindset matters. Unfortunately for me and for my boys, it took me a very long time to understand that before I could change my life, I had to change my mindset.

It seems not only absurd but callous and cruel to hear someone tell you that you need to stop feeling sorry for yourself, or to stop putting negative energy out, when all you ever feel in your life is pain and unfairness. It seems like no one could possibly understand the enormity of your challenges, or they would not tell you to smile through it. But that's because you are so overwhelmed with the amount of chaos and pain and fear and destruction you are experiencing that it seems like a ludicrous suggestion to let go of the only safety net you have—which is built from those things—to take a leap of faith.

Ten years after Lou was killed, I finally hit the very bottom of my ability to exist in the continual shit-show I'd allowed my life to become. The moment I collapsed crying in my driveway on my forty-second birthday was the moment I finally got it.

I finally understood it was going to be up to me to turn life around for myself and my kids. I finally accepted accountability for allowing someone to remain in our lives and wreak the destruction we all experienced. I finally accepted that I'd made the mistake of convincing myself other people were the cause of my failures and that all the terrible things that had happened to me justified my continued misery.

It was a liberating moment.

The person who got back to her feet a few moments later was not the same person who'd fallen to her knees moments ago. Something inside of me had clicked. A switch had been flipped. For the first time in just over ten years since my husband had been murdered, I believed life would be good again. For the first time in my life, I believed I had the power to make that happen.

But how?

That was the hard part. It required taking a complete inventory of my life up until that moment: the times that had broken me and why they'd broken me, how I'd responded to those times, the times that had lifted me and why they'd lifted me, the people in my life at those times, the impact they had on me, the power I allotted them, etc. Then I had to look at the past ten years even harder. I had to put all those things under a microscope and dissect them. I examined my habits and my inner circle and how both of those things impacted me.

I realized I had *a lot* of work to do.

The first thing I did was to change my diet.

Not what I ate or drank so much as what I consumed with my mind and my heart. The personal inventory I conducted revealed that I spent much of my time focused on things that fed my pain and anger. After the kids went to bed, I watched documentaries and movies about crime. Specifically violent crime. I did this while surfing social media and spending time commiserating with other widows who were also stuck in their own pain. But mostly I watched murder shows and read about serial killers. While I was studying for my master's in criminal justice, I'd been able to justify this behavior somewhat. But I'd quickly grown addicted to it. It was like I had to have that fix of negativity and trauma to validate the trauma that continued to dominate my mind.

People who knew me personally may have known about my troubles from a newly ended relationship, but only a few knew the full story behind that, and no one really knew I was still crippled with my unresolved grief and pain from my husband's murder and his killer's acquittal.

The world saw that I'd published two books, been on some national news shows, taken some fun trips, and had the cutest four boys on the planet (in my eyes). They saw social media posts of me partying and smiling and never guessed that when I wasn't swept up in one distraction or another, I was crying alone at night, or while driving, or counting the moments until I could be alone and scream into my pillow. They didn't realize that so much of what they said to me felt like insensitive or uncaring comments. They didn't know that underneath the smile I forced I was telling myself not to expect them to understand. They didn't know I hated family gatherings because it tore me apart to see all the dads with their kids and the husbands with their wives.

No one knew anything about me, really, and I finally stopped blaming them for that.

This sudden achievement of self-awareness was a game-changer. Now that I identified the things I needed to change, my next step was learning *how* to change them.

If I was going to learn how to accept my pain and use it as my ally instead of my enemy, I was going to need to find other people who had done that and learn from them. If I was going to stop feeding my pain and anger, I would have to stop watching violent shows and reading violent books. If I was going to install positivity and change my energy, I was going to have to spend less time with negative people or people who didn't support or understand me and spend more time with people who both supported and understood me. (I go into more detail on this crucial step in a later chapter.) I was going to have to start reading books on mindset and inspirational stories of survival and achievement.

Out with the negative; in with the positive.

Because I struggled with self-esteem issues, I knew I needed to start these lessons by learning from people I would not compare myself to. I needed to find people who were nothing like me but had incredible stories of resilience.

That's when I found Dr. Sean Stephenson and Nick Vujicic.

Dr. Sean Stephenson was given a death sentence just moments after he was born. But this remarkable individual defied his doctors' prognosis first by living, and then by going on to lead an extraordinary life. Osteogenesis imperfecta, or brittle bone disease, is a dangerous, painful condition. This genetic disorder leaves bones vulnerable to breaking with little to no provocation. For Sean, the natural act of being born was enough to crush most of his bones.

"Is this going to be a burden or a blessing?"

This is the question his mother posed to Sean on one of the numerous occasions he found himself writhing in pain on the floor, threatened with the overwhelming pain and futility of his condition.

The question snapped things into focus for him, and Sean learned to assume control of his own response to the life he'd been given.

Pain became his teacher, "… and I was a good little student," Sean Stephenson said when I interviewed him for American Snippets.

When he met someone who pitied him, or flinched or even expressed disgust at him, he turned the sting of their reaction into a boomerang packed with forgiveness and education. He may only have reached three feet in physical height, but he became known as the "Three Foot Giant" because of his huge energy and impact. Before his death in 2019, Sean had interned for a president, earned a certification as a therapist and a doctor of clinical hypnotherapy degree, published books, spoke to global audiences, ran a successful therapy practice, and married the love of his life. He was close friends with some of the top personal development influencers in the world, and I became an avid student of his.

I watched countless YouTube videos of him. I heard him speak in person and I devoured his book, *Get Off Your "But."* Little by little his example became my guide. By the time I interviewed him, I had added dozens more people to my private library of personal development, including Nick Vujicic.

Nick was born with tetra-amelia syndrome, a rare disorder characterized by the absence of arms and legs. Like Sean, the extremeness of Nick's physical appearance caught my eye but the extremeness of his grace and spirit captured my heart. I'm not alone in my appreciation for Nick. He is among the world's most sought-after speakers and he has impacted millions of lives around the world. Nick's candidness, humor, and faith as he openly shares his lessons on heartache, pain, grace, and grit became my go-to along with Sean Stephenson's. I must have watched every video they had out there at the time. I played them every morning before the boys woke, and every night when the boys went to bed.

If you ask me to tell you about any of those videos or cite examples of which parts impacted me most, prepare to be disappointed. I don't actually remember any specifics at all. Not one teeny tiny thing. All I remember is how they made me *feel*. Just like that famous Maya Angelou quote:

"I've learned that people will forget what you said, people will forget what you did, but people will never forget how you made them feel."

When I watched and listened to Sean and Nick, I felt awe. I felt hope. I felt possibility. I felt love. I felt happy. I felt humble and blessed and grateful. What I *didn't* feel was pathetic, or painful, or angry, or any of the other emotions I'd allowed to run my life.My fiancé and I have an expression we like to share with our American Snippets community. If you read my opening to this book, you'll have already seen it, but it's worth repeating. If you skipped my opening, it's a good idea to go back and check it out to maximize the value you receive.

Either way, here it is: "Inspiration without action is just entertainment."

It was great that Nick and Sean inspired me so much. Halting the practice of nurturing negativity had an immediate impact on me and my mood. Emptying my mindset of all the reasons to validate my misery was an absolutely critical first step to changing my life. Replenishing that mindset with positivity was the next important step. But unless I implemented actionable steps to apply those mindset lessons to my own life, I would not move forward in health, finances, achievement, or purpose.

Once I felt like I had a full tank of inspiration, I put the pedal to the metal. I found more people to study and learn from and began expanding the cast of online mentors to include those who'd overcome situations similar to mine. Grief, murder trials (I had to be vigilant about that one so as not to get sucked back into the depressing side of it all), raising kids through grief—I studied those topics obsessively. At some point, I even tossed in watching romantic movies again to remind myself how beautiful love could still be. A bad day was no longer a truly bad day because I always made a point to capture one moment, no matter how small, to prove there is beauty in every day.

I still had a *lot* of messes to clean up. Finding a job this time around was harder than it had ever been before, so I needed to swallow my pride and ask for help. I had to humble myself even more and ask for one last round of help from organizations that support families of fallen service members. I had to get myself on a healthy routine and constantly reinforce the positivity in order to keep the depression and hopelessness from resuming control of my heart.

It was the opposite of easy, but then, just like when you start building muscle tone and getting in shape, I recognized new strength. The mental exercises I did became things I looked forward to instead of forcing myself to do. I followed up on a friend's support to help me qualify for a new career as a Veterans Service Officer, and I met Dave, who I am now engaged to—none of which would have happened if I'd stayed down in the place I'd fallen instead of committing to getting back up.

The road that once looked dark and unforgiving suddenly held a sense of adventure, and I couldn't wait to drive it.

***

Do yourself a favor and do these things today:

- Make a list of all the people you love and don't want to ever lose. Go tell all of those people, today, that you wish them nothing but happiness. If something were to happen to you, you want them to enjoy life anyway.

- Write a letter to each of those people, to be opened in the event of your death. Put the letters somewhere they will be found in that instance.

- Think of those people again. Face the reality that life is temporary for all of us. Either they will lose you, or you will lose them, but there will be loss. You don't have to obsess about it. Just reflect on it and view your time with those people through that new lens. Repeat to yourself that when you lose any of them, you *will* overcome that pain.

- Write down the goals you have and the things you want to happen. Commit to making those a reality but also detach your own idea of happiness from those outcomes. Remind yourself that nothing is guaranteed and that you will overcome any upset or challenge you face.

- Get yourself a copy of Dr. Sean Stephenson's book, *Get Off Your "But."*

- Nick Vujicic has several books out there. Pick up at least one of them.

- Hop online but stay away from the news. Instead, search out people who inspire you and who you resonate with. Make it a habit to watch at least one video or listen to one podcast or read one chapter of a book each day that inspires and teaches you.

Chapter 2
Completing Grief's Incomplete Playbook

The seven stages of grief are neat and tidy, aren't they?

1. Shock
2. Denial
3. Anger
4. Bargaining
5. Depression
6. Testing
7. Acceptance

Seven stages we go through after any loss, really. They are pretty accurate, I'll admit. And yet they are also deceiving and incomplete.

Here's what I mean by that:

Each stage on that list is pretty easy to understand and recognize when you enter it. I remember even as the soldier was uttering the words about Lou's body being positively identified, I wanted to ask him if Lou was okay. I remember thinking it was a mistake, that they got the ID wrong, etc.

And I remember the feelings attached to all the other stages too. But this list … this list does not convey the magnitude of emotions attached to each stage. It does not prepare a person to experience those emotions, and it can lead a person to believe they are not doing it right— that they are not properly grieving. Because very often these stages loop around, overlap one another, and confuse the shit out of you.

The seven stages of grief should become nine stages, with stage eight being forgiveness and stage nine being repeat.

Even after you accept that the loss is real, and work through the depression and anger, it is very likely you cling to regret—regret or guilt for surviving, or about things you did or did not say or do to or with the person you lost, and regret about the things you did or did not do in the aftermath of the loss. That guilt and regret can be a very heavy burden and a big challenge to overcome. Forgiveness to yourself is essential.

After begging and pleading for help from the military, a grief counselor was finally dispatched to my home. I was terrified about leading my children through our tragedy. I was begging God to let me die, and I knew I needed help.

I was what I call actively suicidal. This means I was actively contemplating ending my life. To me, the option had merit for two reasons: it was the only way I would ever escape the merciless pain I was in, and it was the noble thing to do for my kids because they deserved to be raised by someone better and stronger than me.

Even writing these words is difficult now. It takes me back to those moments and memories. It brings me back to my bedroom, sitting on my unmade bed, crying into Lou's pillow while clinging to the fading wisps of his smell on the pillowcase. I can hear the muffled sounds of my four little boys' laughter that hovered around the cloud of my depression. Tiny white tablets vibrated on my fingertips as they tumbled out of the bottle that felt warm in my hand. *Would these be enough to end this for me? Is that really what I wanted? Was it possible that I would one day find a moment's peace from this pain? Was it possible that I was worthy or strong enough to be the leader and mom my boys needed and deserved?*

The answer to all of those questions, at the time, was a resounding NO. I didn't *want* to die. I just wanted the pain to stop. It didn't seem like I was choosing between life or death; it seemed like I was choosing between hell or heaven. I didn't *want* anyone else to raise my boys; I just loved them so intensely that freeing them from me felt like the greatest gift I could give them.

I don't know exactly how I stepped out of that grip of temporary insanity long enough to pour the pills back in the bottle, seal the lid, and stash them in the depth of my drawer. I don't know how to explain the feeling that someone else was actually moving my hands through those motions and implanting the message that the pills were not the solution— ever. All I know is that one second I was a puppet to my pain and the next I was just a prisoner. Not that a prisoner is much better, but at that point it was a step up. Within the span of a moment, I went from feeling like pain was pushing me to end my life to feeling that pain was just the prison I was living in; it may have its bars and high walls, but within those bars and walls was a space for me to live. That would have to do.

Eventually I would graduate into what I call the passively suicidal stage of my own grief. That means instead of actively contemplating killing myself, I would sit under the stars for hours while the kids were asleep and try to command my body to die. All that did was put me in a meditative state that actually wound up calming me. Or I brought a big horse home and hopped on for a reckless ride knowing I would get bucked off. All that achieved was a few moments of unconsciousness and a few weeks to recover from a concussion and severe whiplash, while taking care of four little boys.

Over the months and then the years I would learn that there were indeed days that I would be able to escape that prison of pain, even if only for a moment. I learned that there was a grace in that pain and a path to overcome it. Then I learned I could not only overcome it, but I could harness its power for positive purposes.

But all of that knowledge was light years away from where I sat that day, in my bedroom. In that moment, all I knew was that I needed help. Fast.

It took some time, but when Chaplain Elaine Henderson arrived on my doorstep, she gave me enough strength and insight to carry me through the next months. Some of what she said is seared into my mind.

Over the course of a several-hour session, Elaine walked me through different layers of grief and pain management. It was like an intensive course on faith, resilience, and recovery that crammed years of work into one day. It was brutal and powerful.

At first I didn't want to hear anything she had to say. I held the pillow tighter to myself and struggled to just not pass out because of the traumatic clashing of emotions in my mind and my heart. She patiently walked through that with me until I broke. The tears started and would not stop. I was drenched in them. Elaine pressed on.

We reached a point where I told her about Lou's last calls to me and how I had missed them both. The agony of that, and the guilt and regret, had been crushing me. I told her how I felt guilty for him being there at all—how he'd wanted to join the regular army and I'd made it clear I was not on board with that, so he'd joined the National Guard instead. If only, I said, I had supported his decision to join the army instead of the National Guard, he would never have crossed paths with Martinez.

On I went, listing all the ways I'd failed my husband over the years, until I had run through everything my battered brain could think of at the moment.

Elaine sat quietly through it all. When I was done, instead of telling me what a piece of shit I was like I'd expected, she asked me this:

"In all the time you had with Lou, did you ever do anything intentionally to cause him harm?"

My answer, of course, was a hostile "No."

Well then, she continued, guilt does not apply to any of those things I listed. She went on to explain that all people are fallible, and we all make choices or do things that have unintended consequences. But the only time to feel burdened by the weight of the level of guilt I was carrying, she said, was when the actions were carried out with malicious intent. I had nothing to feel guilty about, she said. She assured me that if she were sitting there with Lou instead of me, he'd have a similar list, and underneath both lists lay a foundation of love. She helped me believe that Lou would forgive me for all of that, and not want me to waste one moment believing otherwise.

This is a paraphrasing of her words, as best as I remember. But the question she asked me about my intent was the thing that shot right through the layers of guilt and shame to free me of both.

Forgiveness helps.

A lot.

The regret is something I admit to still carrying. I may never stop regretting I missed that last call with him—one more chance to say I love you, one more chance to let him know we were okay at home, one more chance, period.

To this day I am obsessive about my phone. It is almost always near me and I am almost always accessible to my friends and family.

I never want to miss a last call again.

To this day those seven stages (nine really) flow in and out of my life. Some days I still don't want to believe it happened. Some days I want to pretend my sons will feel their father's arms around them, know his voice and his laugh, and learn the things he would have taught them. Those moments are actually only seconds, because there is no denying reality. Then the anger storms in and I rage at the unfairness of it all. Then I get depressed, wondering why it still impacts me this way, and then I accept that is just the way it is, but I also need to forgive myself for feeling any of that. I need to forgive myself for feeling like I betray the man who stands beside me and loves me now, whom I also truly love right back. I need to remind myself that loving one does not diminish from the other. After all, I love each of my children with a powerful might, and yet missing one who is away does not devalue or diminish the love I have for any of the others. They all hold a piece of my heart.

It took me a very, very long time to realize that the seven stages should really be nine because we need to forgive ourselves and because the cycle never really ends. It just runs on a loop.

I remember wondering, "What is *wrong* with me?" every time I would feel the cycle starting over, or I would fall back into a stage I thought I'd graduated from. Grief has a beginning, but it has no end.

Once I shifted my mindset to realize I wasn't failing at grief, I was able to begin learning how to manage it.

Many of our guests on American Snippets have traveled their own paths through grief and guilt and pain. Cori Salchert and Bobby Henline are two of those guests whose experiences are so intense and whose insight is so powerful, they need to be shared here.

Cori Salchert is an expert on grief.

Cori, a former bereavement nurse, had spent significant time in her career on the maternity ward, gradually beginning to focus her energy on helping the parents who found themselves in the nightmare of grief instead of taking a healthy baby home from the hospital. One of the biggest impediments to healing for those parents, says Cori, is the general dismissal of the notion that grief applies to a miscarriage.

In a society with so many people who view an unborn child not as a baby, but a lump of disposable tissue, it can be especially hard for parents to find comfort and understanding when a woman loses the baby she is carrying. Cori is fiercely protective of these parents.

"I will fight anyone who says hospice doesn't apply to babies or children in the womb," she warns. "I'm sorry—a family member has died. Someone has been lost. This family needs care for their grief."

When Cori shared this with me during her interview, it struck me hard in a place I'd closed off. Not long after our third son was born, I realized I was pregnant again. This was not necessarily happy news for me, because we had a two-and-a-half-year-old, a one-and-a-half-year-old, and a six-month-old. Lou was a teacher and a National Guard officer, and I was a realtor. We were exhausted and for me, the thought of going through another pregnancy when I felt like I was barely recovered from three in a row was overwhelming, let alone knowing how hard it would be to have another newborn to care for.

I felt like the worst human being for feeling that way, and I hated myself for it. But then I had my doctor appointment, and we heard our baby's heartbeat. With every *thump, thump, thump* echoing from the machine, I felt like my heart was synching up with my baby's, and a wave of love washed over me. I walked into that room exhausted and feeling overwhelmed, but I walked out like I was floating on happiness. So it seemed especially cruel to lose that baby just a few weeks later.

It was just a small spot of blood. Surely it was no big deal, I thought. But I went to the doctor anyway. Lou came with me, with our three little guys strapped on to us or holding our hands. The midwife's face was strained when she met us after the sonogram, which had been unusually quiet. "I'm sorry," she said. "The baby has no heartbeat."

It felt like no one really understood why I was so devastated at this news. Even Lou, who was an amazing and loving father, didn't feel the enormity of this loss like I did. He was sad, but also had been aware of the struggle before us, and maybe felt like we'd been given a reprieve. We both knew we wanted one more baby. We just hadn't expected one so

29

soon. He did his best to assure me we'd try again in a few months, when I was recovered and we were in better shape.

I couldn't stop crying. I cried on the way to the hospital, as they were putting me under, and when I woke up after the procedure. I cried on the way home and in my room. And I felt like no one really got it. After all, we already had three very young kids! Why would we want another?

And I was only three months along—it's not even really a baby yet. Everyone around me seemed to expect me to not be sad. I felt pressure to get back to work, and I wound up sobbing in front of horrified clients before they drove out of my life. Cori was the first person I'd met who made me feel like it was normal to grieve a baby who was only just barely a part of my life.

Cori grew so frustrated at the lack of resources for these parents that she created HALO, the Hope After Loss Organization. The focus was on helping families create whatever good memories they possibly could, whether that meant the feeling of holding their baby— even once— before letting it go, or maybe just swinging on a swing in the park before that baby was born to its death, knowing its medical condition meant it would not survive outside the womb. It is important for people to have one bright moment to hold on to, or many bright moments, when faced with inescapable tragedy. The challenge is in redefining those bright moments. Thanks to Cori, many grieving parents did just that.

Cori learned how to tap into the strength it takes to find that brightness no matter how oppressive the darkness may be. First she did it for others, leading them through their pain. Then she was faced with finding her way through her own life's challenges. A crippling series of autoimmune diseases ganged up on Cori in 2008. These illnesses became so severe they nearly killed her in 2011. The fire within her dimmed. She'd lost her job and her health. Flames of strength turned to embers as her will dissolved and she begged God to die. "Kill me already," she prayed, just like I did. "I don't want to live like this. I don't want to be sick … I'm done." She quit. Tapped out. She wanted to let go. But her husband Mark wouldn't let her.

"Before we have a funeral," he told her, "you're going to try one more time."

With her husband's love and her family's hopes and her own stubborn soul, she found the strength to fight a little more. She found new doctors and new diagnoses. Surgeries restored enough of her body so she could return home and live a long life, but irreparable damage left her unable to work. She turned to God again.

"God, you're going to have to take this mess and redeem it because I don't see any good coming of this at all," she prayed.

Before she'd said goodbye to her work at the NICU, Cori had left word that she'd be willing to help if a family decided they could not care for their baby with a fatal fetal anomaly or a terminal diagnosis. So it was only a matter of time before her phone rang.

The call about the baby born without either brain hemisphere came in the summer of 2012. "Yes," Cori said, without hesitation. "Let's do it," Mark agreed. Hearing that this baby had not even been given a name only stoked their commitment to her. No way, they decided, would this baby be carried out the back door, in a bag, with no one to weep for her. The Salcherts walked into the NICU, past the other babies, straight to the corner with the wooden crib. They saw the tiny, vulnerable infant all by herself.

"Okay," said Cori, "this is not where you belong. We're taking you home."

They named her Emmalynn. Cori's voice brims with tears as she speaks, describing what it had been like to take that baby home and love her for fifty days before she died. "We carried her out the front door. She was chosen and she was cherished. And she has a name and she was known and she is missed and she is still loved." Emotion may threaten to overwhelm her as she shares these memories, but not enough to slow her down or stop her from making sure Emmalynn is remembered. The love Cori still feels for that baby is impossible to miss as she speaks of the happy moments and memories they created.

Emmalyn, once forgotten, lived her short life surrounded by people who loved her and cared for her. She experienced special things like the beach and a concert, and ordinary things, like being taken on errands. "Have baby, have oxygen tank, will travel!" Cori laughs, welcoming the sweet memories even as the painful ones rush back. Emmalynn died in Cori's arms, snug up against Cori's chest, lulled by her

31

heartbeat. She was not alone, and she had been given the gift of experiencing the most from her little life as was humanly possible for Cori and Mark to give to her.

Rather than celebrate on her birthday that year, Cori spent the day planning Emmalyn's funeral. She'd known this would happen—that Emmalyn would die. She understood it and accepted it, and she knew she and her family had done the right thing by reaching past Emmalyn's broken body to touch her soul so she would know she was loved in this life. But that didn't mean it didn't hurt. Emmalyn was no longer in pain, but Cori was.

For three weeks Cori struggled, wondering if she would ever be able to do this for another baby in spite of how much it hurt to lose them. Her family had the answer to that. Mark knew this is what Cori was called to do and her kids knew it, too. They all supported her and they'd all played a role in the care of Emmalyn. Now they pledged their support again, even pushed Cori past her own pain to remind her that she was more or less *supposed* to do this. They all were. "Mom," her daughter asked, "what if there's some kid that needs us and you're just sitting there with a broken heart?" Those words jolted Cori out of her rut, and she realized a broken heart is worth it.

Cori and her family have cared for a host of other children since then. They have nurtured and fussed over little babies otherwise destined to live their short lives literally from cradle to grave, with no light in between. More than once they were able to help a child with a grim prognosis recover from those medical afflictions and find a family to love forever. And more than once they have opened their hearts to love a child, only to endure the grief of that child's death. The Salchert family's decision to accept grief as an unwelcome but inevitable outcome of love has allowed them to develop resilience skills the likes of which few possess.

The Salcherts' extreme grace and resilience in the face of grief serve as strong examples for navigating and overcoming the pain of loss. That's an excellent place to start, but there is much more to grief than the void of loss. The guilt so often experienced by survivors is another powerful component of grief. Bobby Henline knows all about that.

Bobby was on his fourth combat deployment when his Humvee drove over an IED. He was the only survivor. No one really understands how Bobby survived the explosion or his injuries.

The best way he can describe the sensation he had when waking up from a two-week coma is like being on a giant iceberg, with stars everywhere. A lapsed Catholic who had turned toward being an atheist, Bobby recalls that he found God again through that experience, or God found him. "I felt like I was in heaven," he remembers, "and God was telling me I'm not done yet."

Bobby had to rely on the information he got from others to know what happened that day. The last memory he has is of getting coffee that morning. He pieced enough together from firsthand stories and official reports to know that he wasn't even supposed to be in that Humvee. He'd been filling in for someone else.

While everyone else focused on healing or mitigating the damage done from the severe physical injuries he'd sustained, the aftermath of trauma and intense survivor's guilt stealthily overwhelmed Bobby from the inside out. He felt like he did not deserve to be alive. He prayed every night for a year for God to take him. "I felt like a burden to my family. I didn't feel I deserved to live," he said.

Are you picking up on the pattern here?

The obvious losses Bobby suffered were many: he lost an arm, he lost massive amounts of flesh from deadly heat and flames. His face was unrecognizable. He would never look normal again. He entered into years of rehabilitation and surgeries as teams of professionals did their best to help him reclaim his independence and recover from his injuries. Still, the internal anguish continued. His marriage fell apart.

It took him about four years, he says, to learn how to get past most of the hurdles he faced. Eventually he learned how to appreciate life again. He even began to feel good about himself.

Today he's actively involved with helping others navigate their own trauma or tragedies. He and his fiancée built the Bravo748 Speakers Bureau. Bobby also launched his own nonprofit, Forging Forward. Its primary mission is the elimination of suicide among our active duty and military and first responder veterans.

The perspective on guilt that Bobby brings to the table is invaluable.

"I don't think it ever goes away," he says. "It's always kind of there. And I know that I have to live for them." He acknowledges that it still hits him sometimes. His guilt reappears in that loop grief continues to spin on. In those moments, he asks himself the questions that help him regain his balance:

What if I was the one that didn't make it home?

What would I want for the survivor?

Each time he answers the same way:

I'd want that survivor to live their life to the fullest, to chase their dreams, to have a blessed life, to live for us. You know, if I waste my life, if we waste our life, then we're letting them die in vain.

Just like Sean Stephenson's mom taught him to allow the feelings of despair and anger and self-pity be acknowledged but then moved past, Bobby instilled his own rule for his relapses. "Have that pity party. Feel bad. Get it out of your system. But then remind yourself you've got to keep going."

Bobby understands that Forgive and Repeat are part of the process, even if no one teaches them as such. Hearing him confirm what my own experience and so many others' have taught me added that extra validation that I'd identified two missing components to a universal pain: Forgive and Repeat.

Chapter 3
Little Leaders

Children are some of our wisest leaders, if we know how to interpret the wisdom they offer. This is true in all moments, whether tragedy is present or not.

We had kids early in our marriage. Once we started, we didn't stop for a long time.

We had no business starting a family and definitely no business growing one, if you determine that on finances alone. Even with both of us working full time we couldn't afford lot rent for our trailer, so we had to move into a small cottage his sister owned. Yes, that's right—he was a teacher at a Catholic high school. I was a manager at a humane society. And we couldn't afford $300 a month for lot rent.

So we had a baby. And then we had another one and brought our ten-month-old son and our one-month-old infant with us to bankruptcy court. And then we had two more kids. Stress was not difficult to come by even before tragedy hit, but even in those stressful times, when I allowed myself to sit back and simply be present, our children introduced joy into those moments.

By the time our youngest was born, we'd rolled through that bankruptcy, had a car repo'd, got an apartment, lost the apartment, moved in with my parents, and then managed to buy our own home. In between all that, 9/11 occurred and Lou's National Guard duty felt more like regular military life. He was gone for months on end and I was alone with the four boys, the house, and my own career to manage. Still, they were happy times, and it was not difficult for me to find fun moments with the boys. They adored me at that point in their lives. I was their rock star, and we could always make each other laugh more than any of them would cry. Mostly.

But when tragedy struck and Lou was killed, I forgot for a moment to be open to their wisdom. First I collapsed to the point that our youngest was afraid of me. Then I rallied and became so focused on leading them, on protecting them from anything unpleasant, that I forgot to remember that they had insight to offer simply by being themselves.

I got my first reminder a couple months later.

It was a sticky summer day, and I had a break from my widow duties. Many days my Casualty Assistance Officer (CAO) would appear to deliver some form of pain to me, or to drive me to a different form of a painful experience. But that day there was no trip to a funeral home to sign papers, no trip to West Point to get my widow ID. There was no trunk of Lou's personal items being delivered, no bank account to remove his name from, and no calls planned with the prosecution team. There was just time alone with my kids. Trevor was six and Colin was five. Sean had just turned four and Jeremy was about a month shy from turning two.

I had all the kids outside with me, enjoying the warm weather. They were on the swings, riding bikes in the driveway, climbing trees, and playing with the dog.

With the youngest on the swing, my mind wandered off. I began letting grief permeate the moment. Suddenly I felt a splash on my arm. Then another, and another. I became aware that the blue skies had turned almost black, and rain was kicking in.

"C'mon inside guys," I called to the kids as I swooped Jeremy from the swing.

"Mom, come here!" I heard a voice come back to me through the now driving rain and wind. I traced the voice to our trampoline. My three oldest kids were jumping around in the rain, sliding and falling on the slick surface. Their laughter seemed to drown out the wind.

"Come on mom! Bring Jeremy on with us!"

By now all five of us were drenched. The air was still warm, and the rain felt even warmer. But nothing warmed me more than the sound of my kids laughing in the rain. So I hopped on with Jeremy and joined the party.

If I close my eyes and concentrate, I can still hear that laughter now. I can smell and feel the rain, and I can hear the boys and me yelling at the top of our lungs, whooping it up.

I don't remember how long we stayed out there. Long enough for the summer storm to pass and the sun to reclaim the sky. Eventually we

36

were laughed out and the kids were hungry, so we got off the trampoline and I told them I'd bring them all towels and snacks outside.

On an impulse, I picked Trevor up and slid him back and forth across the table outside to dry it off. He and I still snicker at the memory today. The laugh coming from him and his brothers as their crazy mother used him as a towel rammed it home to me:

There is power in play. There is power in laughter. It is possible to laugh and feel joy, even for a moment, in spite of pain.

Every moment I was able to find true laughter was one more moment I stole back from grief. Every fun memory I created with my kids was one less opportunity for sadness to rule their day.

Trampoline Rain is one of the happiest memories for all of us. The tradition lives on today. Less often, for sure, but when we do seize the moment, the joy is the same.

Without my children forcing me to keep moving every day, I am fairly convinced I would have curled up in a ball and made no effort to reclaim joy, at least for some time. But my kids reminded me that hearts want to be happy, and moods can be determined for ourselves sometimes.

Imagine if I'd told the boys no. Imagine if I'd told them to get off that trampoline and get inside out of the rain. I would have missed that moment that turned into magic for them and for me. And I would never have known the joy of Trampoline Rain.

Sometimes we have to dig deep to come through for our children. This has certainly been true for all loving parents for all of time, and it became more so for me after tragedy. One such moment took on a particularly absurd form that taught me although a playful spirit may not always be easy to maintain, it is worth it.

We found out that the first hearing for the soldier who killed Lou and Phil would be held on Halloween. In Kuwait.

There was no way I would miss one single appearance by this traitor to make sure he knew I was going to watch him die one day. But to do that I would have to skip out on Halloween with the kids.

I never got into Halloween. To me it was really just an expensive pain in the ass. Buying bags of candy to give away, buying costumes because I suck at being crafty, and shepherding small children through the often cold, dark Halloween weather, up and down stairs to houses, through wet lawns and then hearing one complain that someone else got better candy was never something I looked forward to. That was Lou's jam and he loved doing it. But that year I did not want to have the kids feel like they got robbed of another moment.

This required a plan, and one soon presented itself to me.

Lou's hometown was holding a Halloween parade the weekend before Halloween. I would be able to get in costume with the boys, walk in the parade, and take them trick-or-treating in that small celebration area before I left for Kuwait.

It was a perfect solution.

Star Wars was the thing in our home then. All of them loved it. Light sabers were regularly brandished at me, at each other, at the dog— whatever or whoever. The theme music was sure to get them riled up at any moment, and they jumped at my offer to order whatever Halloween costumes they wanted.

In a few days, a large box arrived. In it was a pile of costumes. Jedis, stormtroopers, Darth Vader, and one authentic Chewbacca costume. The boys tore into them, and I helped Jeremy put his costume on before I snuck into the bedroom with mine.

Outside my door I heard them belting out the Star Wars theme, clanking light sabers, and jumping on the couch. I could barely contain my own grin as I climbed into that Chewbacca costume one piece at a time. A glance through the eye slits (which were in the nostrils of the costume) let me see enough of myself in the mirror to know it looked exactly like Chewbacca, with the dangling fur and all.

Doing my best impression of Chewbacca's yell, I lumbered into the living room to join the boys.

Instantly, the yelling intensified and light sabers pounded me amidst peals of laughter. I couldn't see and hadn't figured out how to move well yet, so I just stood still laughing inside that costume, congratulating myself on bringing more laughter to the boys and me.

Until I heard the scream.

Jeremy, now two years old, was screaming his head off, and not with joy. The poor little guy was terrified of Chewbacca. I took the mask off to let him see it was me, and his eyes popped out. Then a look of betrayal crept onto his face.

"Why you do that mommy?" He chastised me. The other boys thought it was hysterical. Jeremy, not so much.

The parade was a week away and Jeremy was petrified of the costume. I had a problem with only one remedy:

For the next six days, the costume either hung in the living room where he could examine it closely, or I wore it in pieces. One day a car drove by, and I noticed all the occupants staring at me. What are they looking at? I wondered.

The car crept to a halt. Phones came out and pointed at me. What the… I wondered again, before I remembered I was wearing that freaking costume. Right beside me was my two-year-old son in his stormtrooper costume, minus the mask he refused to wear. He was chatting away like two-year-olds do, fully accustomed to the costume at that point.

I'm not sure what the people in that car were thinking as they drove away, but I know what I was thinking—victory! My son was finally used to the costume and we would all be able to walk in the parade.

For me, walking in that parade with all my children was the first challenge I felt I'd handled well for them. It was the first moment I felt an ounce of hope that I would be able to work through their fears and come out the other side with them.

It was a victory achieved through absurdity, but it was a victory nonetheless. I was short on those at the moment, so I took that one and put it in my pocket to save for a rainy day.

Jeremy wasn't trying to teach me anything in that instance. He was two. The only thing he wanted to teach me at that time was the name of every train in Thomas the Train.

But he taught me anyway, and he led me through a very stressful, anxious time by presenting me with something to focus on other than the fact that I would soon be in Kuwait, in the same room as the Being who murdered my husband.

Leaders aren't always aware that they are leading. Lessons aren't always obvious. But if we open our hearts to them, lessons are everywhere. Even in a Chewbacca costume.

Holidays are hard when you lose someone you love. The trip to Kuwait completely drained me. I was glad I'd gone, but the horror of testimony I'd heard, the energy of being in the room with a killer—the entire experience overloaded me. Additional experiences with items missing from Lou's things, messages from people who'd been there, anticipation of hearings and everyday efforts of caring for four children while gripped in massive depression had me pretty convinced the holidays were going to be awful.

If I was going to have any shot at getting through Christmas without Lou, I'd have to skip Thanksgiving, which was a favorite for him, and have someone else unpack the decorations he'd packed up so carefully the year before. And a tree? Hell no! No way was I going to get and decorate a tree without Lou!

Feeling guilty but still sure the kids would have a better Thanksgiving experience without me, I fled to Arizona and spent Thanksgiving on a mountain with my sister and brother. I returned home to a fully decorated Christmas tree, courtesy of Lou's family.

My breath caught as the lights twinkled gently in the dark. There was the silver star Lou loved, instead of the angel I preferred. We swapped each year, and that year the star seemed to scream of Lou's presence. I could hear him gloating in my mind, explaining why the star was better than the angel. It made me smile before it made me want to vomit.

There was the NY Rangers ornament he loved. He was a raging fan of the Rangers and that ornament was something he cherished. I stood for a moment, staring at it.

Trevor walked over beside me. I crouched down to give him a hug. When he stepped out of the hug a moment later, his arm popped out and hit that ornament.

Tink! It wasn't a loud sound when the ornament shattered, but it felt as loud as the shot that was heard around the world. I froze in place, feeling the bile rising in my gut as I saw something precious to Lou—a link to him—shattered.

The only one more horrified than me was Trevor. Tears exploded from his big blue eyes, his little lips shook, and his terrified voice apologized as fast as it could.

In that moment, another lesson was learned:

Objects are just that—objects. They may be a reminder of a time or a place or a person, but the true link to that memory lies within us, not within any object.

We can obsess on objects—we can guard possessions as if they are the only tie that binds us to something or someone we hold dear. But it is inevitable that objects will break or be lost or lose their glow, and then what?

I pulled Trevor back into a hug and told him it was okay, fighting to not let him see me cry as I struggled with losing the ornament. At the same time, though, I felt released from its power that I didn't even know it held over me.

Trevor did me a favor in that moment. He taught me to never give power to an object. Never need a possession to the point that you are lost without it. A home, a car, a book, a wedding ring—I've said goodbye to all of those things over the years. They all held a tie to Lou, and I felt like I lost a piece of him when I said goodbye to those things, but only for a moment.

But that is the reality of life and change. To be free to flow into each day, we have to be free of what holds us to the past. We have to be free to accept what comes next and take comfort in holding feelings in our hearts over objects in our hands.

Ever since that ornament smashed, I have reminded myself over and over that no matter what else I lose—objects or even some memories—nothing changes the feelings I can hold on to. The only thing we leave this life with is our soul, and my soul doesn't need a Christmas ornament to be blessed with the feelings of love that will never fade.

Life is hard. No doubt about that. But it does not have to be harder than circumstances warrant, and there should always be moments to celebrate. No one makes celebrating easier than kids. They will celebrate anything if given the chance.

The last day of the school year is something every child looks forward to, and it seems like a great opportunity to let the kids have a party with a few of their friends.

I started the tradition with my two oldest sons in second and third grades officially inviting their friends over. My two youngest hung out with my two nephews who were the same age, live within two miles of us, and were happy to join the party. Their moms are two of my sisters (I have four sisters and two brothers) as well as teachers, so they were also in the party mood.

It started off totally manageable the first year. I got 100 cans of silly string, filled a couple hundred water balloons, grilled some hot dogs and hamburgers, and my sisters and I launched our assault on the boys as they tumbled off the bus.

There was an inflatable water slide for the smaller kids and the pool for the bigger kids. Tents were pitched and about a dozen boys slept over.

It was a great day. I just never anticipated what would happen the following year.

After that first party, word spread. My kids came home from the first day of school the following September and told me they'd already been asked about the last day party!

I was like … uh oh.

That party grew and grew, until one night I was alone with forty kids sleeping over. We had check-in and sign-out lists for parents to sign, having had a mishap one year with one parent not knowing her kid caught a ride with a friend.

Oops.

We had lifeguards and assigned pool times for the kids based on what class they were in, when about seventy kids showed up one year.

One friend's dad had an ice cream business. One year, right at midnight, he surprised us with his ice cream buffet of flavors and toppings..

It was sweet and gave me a break, until he left and I was alone with mayhem.

One kid ate about a gallon of ice cream. I know this because that's approximately what I cleaned up in the bathroom after it exploded out of both ends.

Exhausted, and with the kids settled in tents far enough from me that I couldn't hear them farting or telling dirty jokes, I snuggled onto the glider swing on the patio where I could still see the tents.

Slowly, I drifted into a light sleep, then wham! A visiting skunk annihilated me.

That was the last year the party was a sleepover.

That party tradition may have been crazy, but it was also important. It gave my kids the chance to shirk off the stress for a moment and just be kids. It gave me something to focus on instead of my pain. And it reminded me of the impact we have on our kids.

Again, my kids were not trying to teach me anything with this. But they taught me anyway. They taught me that applying time and effort to something positive elevates your mood, which is vital to people struggling with depression. They taught me that every milestone should be celebrated even though someone important is missing from our lives. They taught me that we can still create joy in spite of pain, and they taught me to never, ever, have an open-bar ice cream party for kids at midnight.

One of my hardest memories is a conversation I had with Lou about a month before he left. You know those moments that burn themselves into your brain? The ones where you remember every detail, from the lighting to any smells to the feel of a fabric and the sound of a voice?

This is one of those moments. While I don't remember the entire conversation, I do vividly remember the most painful part.

The sun hit Lou in slivers of light blended with the shadows from tree branches as we stood on our back porch. I remember the way he leaned on the rail and tilted his head up to catch the beams of light. I remember what he was wearing: his white t-shirt with NY Yankees written in cursive on it, shorts, and Sambas.

I don't remember how the conversation evolved. I just remember the most powerful parts.

We were talking about worst-case scenarios, cautiously circling the topic of potential for Lou to be killed in Iraq. Both of us agreed that it would be even harder for either of us to lose one of our children than each other, but Lou then seemed like he was struggling with another concept.

43

"It would really suck," he said, "if I die when they are still so young, and they don't remember me or know how much I love them."

"I never want you or the kids to visit a cemetery to see me," he said. "If something happens to me, cremate me, scatter me, pour some beers and toast me."

He said this in a voice I'd never heard before, as if he was clenching his teeth and pushing those words past boulders caught in his throat.

The conversation lasted maybe three or four minutes, and we changed the topic and moved on. He never spoke of that subject again. He refused to. But it stayed with me.

Even as I write this, all these years later, this memory is one that just opens the floodgates. Literally, I am crying on my laptop right now, and on the cat who is laying on my lap as I write. That's how much that moment hits me every time.

It hit me then too. It hit us both. Lou was not a crying kind of guy, but when he said those words that day on our porch, he closed his eyes and his voice broke, and I felt my own world spin for a moment at the thought.

It absolutely destroys me if I dwell on those couple hours he had between injury and death, and those moments in which he knew the very fears he voiced were about to become a reality.

I made it my mission to do everything I could to make sure the boys held on to as much of their dad as possible.

They will never fully understand how hard he worked to support us all. They will never remember how all-in he was with us and they will never know what it is like to have him guide them through life, but I was hell-bent on making sure they know he loved them.

Our youngest wasn't even two years old when Lou died. Our oldest was six. I knew they would have either no memory of him at all or very vague memories at best. All I could do when the older boys cried because they forgot what his voice sounds like was tell them it was okay—that they were not doing anything wrong and their dad would understand. But what they could do instead was simply close their eyes and think of happy things and know that is what their dad was about.

All I could do was make sure they associated love with the word dad, because they would not have any memories to attach to the word. All I could do was make sure the word dad evoked a smile and a feeling of love instead of a gravestone and pain.

I took them to the cemetery once.

Jeremy leapfrogged from stone to stone, peering in the planters. The other three stood there, confused and unsure what to do. So did I. It was awkward and unnatural, and I knew I would never force them to come back. I knew he deserved to be remembered as a living, breathing, source of love—not as a cold stone in the ground. (Sidenote: I realize this is not a universal mindset or approach. I see people visiting cemeteries regularly, bringing balloons for birthdays and daughters in prom gowns posing by their father's headstone—we all navigate grief differently. We all find our own way to balance pain and love, and no one method is right or wrong.)

So although I regularly asked them if they wanted to go to the cemetery, they always said no. I made sure they knew I would take them anytime they wanted, but they still said no.

Instead, I showed them pictures of their dad. I talked about how he loved them and how hard he worked. I shared stories of our arguments and our laughter, and I did all I could to make sure that even if they had no solid memories, they knew Dad = Love.

I felt powerless to do anything else.

I also realized how tenuous all of our lives are and that there is nothing preventing some crazy tragedy from ending my own life at any moment. Having pushed through the major depression, I now had told myself I could do whatever I wanted with myself or to myself later, after the boys were grown, but for now they needed me and this is where I'd be.

What could I do, then, to make sure they all had at least one vivid, beautiful memory of me? Something they could pull out for the rest of their lives, and remember and smile and remind themselves that no matter how bad things got, or how I'd let them down or whatever else happened, I loved them so strongly?

What age would they have to be to have that experience and remember it?

That's how the Eight-Year-Old Escapades came to life.

One outrageously awesome day with each boy any time between their eighth and ninth birthdays. I had twenty-four hours to fit in an experience they would remember forever, with just me and them. Each experience involved flight of some kind. I'd wake them up before the sun rose or I'd make an announcement as they were about to get on the bus. "Surprise! It's your Escapade Day!" And off we would go.

Trevor was first. We had a car service take us to JFK, a flight to upstate New York, and a tour of the New York and Canadian sides of Niagara Falls. We got drenched in the tunnel behind the Falls, ate lunch at the top of a building, and made memories to last. The only glitch of the experience was the driver.

The driver that showed up in the dark of pre-dawn, on a morning draped in fog, was well beyond retirement. His hands shook so hard—I shit you not—that the steering wheel shook with them and I spent both drives—yes, he also showed up to drive us home—petrified that we were about to crash.

The other three boys got limos. Sorry, Trevor.

There was a sunrise hot air balloon ride and a limo to Six Flags, a limo to the city with a helicopter ride over Manhattan and a Broadway show, and a limo ride to Philadelphia to hop in a biplane for a soar through the skies before a day at the zoo.

Extravagant? Yup.

A waste of money? Hell. No.

By the time I paid off one Escapade it was time for the next and I just rolled it into my budget for about four years. The one-on-one time with each of my sons was priceless and yes, they remember each one. Come what may, they will always have that memory, and so will I.

I moved into Eighteen-Year-Old Escapades, pledging a week of travel one-on-one with each son during their spring break in their freshman year of college. Trevor and I made it to Iceland and those memories would fill many pages. I am now two years behind on Colin and about to be a year behind on Sean, having let responsibilities delay me, but they are patient and their Escapades still await.

So what did those Escapades teach me and what is the lesson for you?

There is a balance to be struck between being fiscally responsible, and letting finances stand between you and momentous experiences. Plan accordingly. Make the moment happen and you will not regret it.

Life is tenuous and we are all on unknown timelines. If there is something you want to do, something you want to make happen, do it. Make it happen. Do not let excuses or fear or anger be the things that stop you. The best day to start any adventure is today. Start visualizing it. Map out a plan, and then execute the plan to make it happen.

There are mentors and YouTube videos to teach you what you need to know. There are gazillions of ways, last time I counted, to make extra money and to save money, to pay for that thing or that moment that will last a lifetime, and for which the ripple effects will be felt for years.

But that's not to say that special moments have to come with a hefty price tag.

I used to have Special Days with the kids too.

You and I would call them mental health days.

Because they all did well academically, the boys would play hooky with me on occasion, and I was not worried about their grades. One at a time I would keep them each home, two-to-three times a school year. We would spend time together doing nothing special and then do something fun. Maybe they would come on errands with me and I would let them pick their favorite snacks at the store. Or we'd find a nice park to picnic or hike in, or a movie to go to. Or we would light a fire in the fireplace and rent a movie, or we'd play a board game or some ping-pong. Just goof off and let them enjoy some downtime while I enjoyed them.

Special Days are something I believe all parents should do with their kids at least once a year, and preferably more. Especially for those parents with more than one child. This gives them the chance to have your undivided attention and lets them know they are, well, special to you.

Every moment matters, but not every moment is going to feel good. Why not create as many good memories with the people you love while you still can? You never know when memories will be all you have left.

Tucking the boys in could take as long as two hours every night. They all wanted their mom to spend time comforting them and talking with them as they unwound from the day—they deserved it. They each had their own technique and no matter how exhausted I was, I made it a point to take that time with each of them in the first months after Lou was killed.

Sean was the one I dreaded this with—not because I love him less, but because he made me use strength I didn't know I had every single night.

"Mom," he'd whisper as he grabbed my hand. With his hazel eyes that are exact replicas of Lou's, he'd stare right into my soul. His cheeks, chubbier than anything else on his skinny little body, would lift as he smiled full of hope. "I wished on the star again tonight, Mommy. This time I know it will work. This time my wish will bring Daddy back."

While every part of me wished it was true and wanted to do anything to avoid crushing that beautiful soul, the other part of me believed I'd do him much more harm than good if I let him believe it.

So before I'd enter his room each night I'd pray for the strength to do what needed to be done.

"Oh Seanie," I'd tell him, "Remember how I told you that it's impossible for Daddy's body to hold his soul anymore? Remember how I told you his soul went to Heaven with the angels? How Daddy will now only be able to visit us in our hearts, and we won't see or hear him like we used to?"

I'd watch his lips start to quiver and his eyes start to water. He'd bite his lip and blink his eyes and let my hand go as he forced a fake smile and said, "That's alright Mommy. I'll wish again tomorrow."

And I'd kiss him good night and tell him I loved him and sob by myself in the quiet house.

This was one of the hardest lessons I had to learn—how to do what had to be done no matter how much it hurt. I knew that giving Sean false hope would be far crueler than hard truth. Each night I left his room my heart would at once feel like it was newly shattered and slightly restored. It made me realize how difficult the rest of life was going to be and it also made me realize I had more strength than I believed I did—and my kids brought that out in me.

Those of us lucky enough to have kids can turn to our love for them as an opportunity to discover and build our own inner strength. Sean didn't mean to teach me that lesson. None of my kids did. But they taught me just the same.

***

I'm blessed with great friends. Two of these friends own an eighty-acre horse farm that I spent years working on. The farm served as a bed and breakfast and wedding venue as well.

At the time Lou was killed, all of their guest cottages were fully booked. Knowing I needed an escape from our home that was filled with reminders of the life we'd lost, my friends offered to let me and my four boys stay in their largest cottage for as long as we'd like.

I had no idea they kicked guests out and canceled on others to make this happen.

It was a gift to spend the days and nights there. In the daytime I'd wander the farm with my kids. We'd play with the mini horses, take adventures along the paths, moo at the cows, and ride bikes and scooters. I'd also hop on a horse and take each of my boys on individual rides with me.

One of the things I struggled with most—that had me most stuck— was wishing they'd had Lou to raise them instead of me because he had so much to offer and I had … nothing. But one day I popped my five-year-old son Colin in the saddle with me, and we strolled the property. Soft trots and slow lopes had us both feeling a rush of fun. As we returned to the paved driveway, the sound of the horse's iron-shod hooves made the clip-clop sound often heard in movies or on TV in horse scenes.

It was one of my favorite sounds. The faint smell of horse sweat, mixed with fresh-cut grass, was a favorite scent. In the saddle with me was one of my favorite people and what he said next was a game-changer for me: "I love that sound Mommy, the sound the horse makes when he walks." As he said this, he leaned back into me, swinging his legs with carefree movement.

In that moment I realized I'd given my son a moment he savored. My passion for horses and love of life on the farm turned into a retreat of sorts, full of moments he'd experience new things.

Colin is very music- and rhythmic-oriented—the steady beat of the horse's hooves was like music to him, and he was soaking it all in.

It was right then and there that I realized I do have the ability to provide value to my kids' lives. I do have the ability to lead them into joyous moments and new opportunities. Maybe, I thought, I'd find more things I was good at, or had experience with, that I could teach my kids. Maybe they weren't doomed with me as their only surviving parent.

That moment didn't put a magical end to all my doubt and concerns or squash my pain. But it did push it back long enough for me to see behind that curtain to a world where I was a good, strong, fun mom that my boys would be safe and well with.

My son wasn't trying to teach me anything. That's what makes these lessons so powerful: that they are present in our lives and can come from people who aren't even aware of the lesson they are teaching.

We never know how our words or actions may inspire, move, or impact someone. Something we casually do or say, which we consider just an extension of ourselves, may be a game-changer for someone else.

That day, taking Colin for that horseback ride changed his day by giving him that special time. I had no idea he was going to love it so much, or remember it still today, all these years later. Colin saying what he said to me was the first time hope penetrated my fear, and it is a moment I fall back to in my mind when I doubt what I have to offer my children.

***

"When are you going to make a whole chicken again?" asked Trevor. I had my back to him when he asked this, as I was sliding a tray of chicken fingers into the oven. He was sitting at the kitchen table doing his homework, his feet kicking under his chair and oblivious to the gut punch he'd just delivered.

It was around five months after Lou had died. Making any dinner at all was a victory for me but making one of Lou's favorite meals was out of the question.

Roast chicken is a simple thing that has a way of becoming something bigger. To me it was about the smell that accompanied the homestyle meal with mashed potatoes and a pile of butter. Lou and I always loved cold winter afternoons with the smell of a roasting chicken and a fireplace glowing with flames. The chicken soup made with leftovers was another favorite of his.

I had just learned how to make it through a trip to the grocery store without crying as I bypassed all those favorite items of his I'd never buy for him again. The thought of that chicken was overwhelming, and I wanted to burst into tears when Trevor asked me this, but instead I chose an honest answer.

"Well, buddy," I said as I walked over to him and looked him in the eye. "You see, roast chicken was one of your dad's favorites, and it just makes me so sad to make it without him."

Trevor, in his six-year-old wisdom, thought that over for a minute. His eyes clouded for a split second before he shook his head and shook that nonsense right out. "Mom," he said, "we can't go forever without ever having chicken again!"

To be clear, Trevor probably had the closest bond with Lou. He was our oldest and he was Lou's sidekick pretty much every minute Lou was home. For months, Trevor would dissolve into tears every time the sun set because it reminded him of Daddy's soul going up to heaven. We had to go inside and close every curtain. He was in no way over losing his dad, or in no way all better. He was just a small child who also loves a good roast chicken and the chicken soup that follows, and the thought of one more thing he enjoys being taken from him seemed cruel and unjust.

It both broke my heart and swelled it with love when he said those words to me. I tousled his hair, kissed his head, and promised him I'd get that chicken the next time I shopped.

The next morning, I forced myself to drive to the store while the boys were in school and daycare. When the smell of roasting chicken greeted Trevor home, it was like the happiest of Christmas mornings. "Mom! You did it! You made a chicken!" he yelled.

The other three had no real idea what Trevor was so happy about, or why Mom's half-broken smile seemed slightly less broken for a moment. They just seemed happy to feel joy swirling in the air.

That chicken was one of the most delicious I've ever tasted, and that dinner was one of my happiest with my four little nut jobs.

What did it teach me, and what can it teach you?

Life is for the living may be a cliché, but clichés exist for a reason. Most types of heartache and tragedy are going to hold a baseline of pain that will always be present in varying degrees. To add to that baseline by denying ourselves even one moment of joy or discontinuing practices that once brought us joy is asinine, really. Think about it. Have you ever broken up with someone and then never gone back to a restaurant you used to go to together? If you lose your job today does that mean you will never watch your favorite Netflix series again?

Why do we deprive ourselves of things we enjoy because we experience something hurtful? Why would we remove one moment of relaxation and peace from ourselves when we are at maximum stress levels?

It makes no sense and yet we all do it.

Next—and this is a repeat of a previous lesson—all hearts want to feel joy. Some lessons bear repeating, and this is one. We may think we want to die but in reality, we just want the pain to stop. We want to be happy, but we don't believe this is possible for us. Kids are the absolute best at teaching us how to disappear into a moment. In a nanosecond, they can go from crying to laughing, and they can turn any moment into a powerful memory just like that.

They are little but they are leaders, even when they don't mean to be. It is our own loss if we do not open our heads and our hearts to their insight.

Who are the little leaders in your life? Are they your children? Your nieces and nephews, or grandchildren? Are they your neighbors or your friends' kids? Do yourself a huge favor and spend time around them as much as possible. Go sit in a park and watch kids play if you have no other kids in your life. Turn your phone off and simply be in that moment with them or around them. Watch the way they notice tiny things we all overlook. Listen to the way they laugh with every drop of their souls, and how they cry the same. Observe how they are 100% committed to each moment as they live it.

You were like that once. You noticed ladybugs on benches and splashed in puddles. You danced without caring who was watching.

Hold on to those lessons those little leaders are teaching you by example. Wrap them up in your heart, preserve them in your mind, and use them accordingly in life.

When you are convinced everything around you is awful, or you have nothing to be excited about, shrink your vision. Sit on the floor if you can, and simply look around you. Note the way the light hits a certain object. Enjoy the feel of that soft shirt on your skin, or the slight burn of a stretch. Laugh at the sound your knees make if they pop when you get back up. Whatever. Think small. Inward. Marvel at the very many wonders we all overlook and let that little girl or boy inside of you dance.

Chapter 4

Dead Puppies Aren't Much Fun—The Dangers of Hiding Pain Behind Distractions

Our brains have very primitive but very strong defense mechanisms. All sorts of studies exist to teach us about those defense mechanisms. Fight or flight is among the most notable differences in the mechanisms of self-defense.

I've deployed both of those tactics against pain and learned a lot about them in the process.

In this chapter we will focus on flight.

I fled from every drop of pain I could by using things to distract me. Alcohol, humor, parties, men, and—puppies. Not necessarily in that order.

Let's get to the puppies first.

My initial canine addition to our lives after loss was for protection. As much as I loved our black Lab mix, three-year-old Cassie was not big enough or tough-looking enough to make us feel a measure of safety.

Safety, for my boys especially, was huge.

In the weeks after learning a bad guy killed daddy—and that the bad guy was really one of our very own soldiers— trust and safety became a focal point for my little boys. One day I saw Styrofoam peanuts placed around every living room window as well as the door.

Those, my sons explained, were bombs. If daddy was killed by a traitor, how were we supposed to protect ourselves? How would we know who was good or bad, or how could we stop anyone from breaking in and killing us? If any bad guy tried to come in here, the bombs would kill them first.

I had my work cut out for me, that's for damn sure.

Overwhelming feelings of helplessness and vulnerability dominated our lives. We all felt it and it was among the first priorities in my life to find a way to help my kids feel safe in their own home.

For weeks, I scoured the internet in search of a trained protection dog that could double as a family dog. I wanted a dog my kids could cuddle with but one that would also shred a person limb from limb if that person attempted to hurt my kids. On command only, of course.

Seemed like a reasonable enough expectation to me at the time.

If I made that same search today, I'd probably find several potential candidates to love and protect us. I'd probably even find someone who would help me acquire said canine for little to no cost and help the boys and me build a trusting bond with our dog before turning us loose with each other.

But in 2005–2006, no such options existed within my search. The closest I came was a company that would provide a dog for the small fee of $25,000.

So I hopped on another search and signed on to adopt a mastiff mix puppy from the South.

Within days the boys and I met the rescue puppy's transport driver in the parking lot of a local grocery store. The rescue van door opened, and a cute little pit bull/bulldog-mix-looking puppy peered out at me, but no mastiff mix was present.

Realizing I'd again been lured out to see a breed I wasn't looking for (our Lab mix was supposed to be a Rottweiler mix), I sighed and accepted the ball of mutt into our home and into our hearts, fully expecting to love this dog as much as we loved Cassie.

Yoda was mostly white with a patch on his eye. Over the next six months, he grew to about 65 lbs. and underwent two eye surgeries to correct the condition I hadn't been told he had. He certainly looked intimidating already, and he was still a puppy.

For the most part he was a gentle soul, but on occasion, I'd catch him almost stalking my youngest son Jeremy. After his eye surgeries, it was as if he saw Jeremy for the first time. There was something about how Yoda would go stone still and lock his gaze on Jeremy when my son ran and squealed like two-year-olds do that made me uncomfortable.

Then Yoda got to Jenny.

Jenny was the rabbit we'd adopted. My friend raised rabbits for meat, which I hadn't realized, I guess. I happened to arrive on the day the rabbits were about to be loaded up and sent to market and, long story short, I came home with about fourteen rabbits right about the time I was heading to Kuwait.

We got them all adopted out before my trip, but Jenny—there was something special about the little brown bunny that we couldn't resist. She'd hop over for head scratches, follow us around, and chill out on our laps.

Jenny joined our family and that was that.

One day I left her in a portable pen on the lawn while I aired out her indoor cage. It was a beautiful day, and Jenny was digging it, so I extended her outdoor time. The two dogs were tucked in their fenced area outside as well and everything was just fine, or so I thought.

Everything was not fine.

Apparently, the sight of Jenny frolicking in her pen triggered Yoda's prey drive. He attacked the gate of the dog enclosure, snapped the latch, and bore down on poor Jenny, who never stood a chance.

We were devastated, and Yoda became public enemy #1.

This is where I began to stray down the path of distraction as a diversionary tactic for pain.

Imagine for a moment: four little boys whose father had been murdered, and whose mother was beside herself in grief, half out of it many days. These little boys had moved from their family home, started a new school (Trevor and Colin were in first grade and kindergarten; Sean and Jeremy were in preschool), and had grown very attached to both Jenny the rabbit and Yoda the dog.

Now Yoda, whom we all trusted (they all trusted explicitly, even though I'd begun keeping an eye on him), had betrayed that trust and attacked and killed poor innocent Jenny, who'd thought she was safe in her pen.

Sound like a familiar theme?

You could hear unhealed wounds being gouged even deeper almost as loudly as you could hear the kids crying.

It was more than I could manage on top of the guilt I felt from being the one who'd left Jenny out in her pen.

Sigh.

There was only one thing to do.

We got another rabbit to fill the empty space and distract us from our pain.

This one was an Angora and looked nothing like Jenny. I don't remember its name, so I'll call him George.

George looked like a slipper. He was nowhere near as friendly as he was cute, but he served as a distraction and that is what I'd been desperate for, so all was well.

This time we got a big bulky rabbit pen made of thick metal on the outside frame and a secure solid flooring. There was no way Yoda could get to George even if he did find an opportunity to try.

I reinforced the dog fence too—or our neighbor did—and believed all bases were covered. Yoda had been placed on probation. Kids have forgiving hearts.

George enjoyed an indoor/outdoor life, hopping around the living room a few hours a day with us and then being tucked into the Fort Knox rabbit hutch the rest of the time.

And then it happened. Yoda was ten months old, approaching 80 lbs. of solid muscle, when he tore apart the dog fence again and bent the metal frame of that hefty rabbit pen to expose the wood. He tore through the wood, ripped open the wire, and tore poor George apart piece by piece.

Our neighbor Keith found the poor rabbit somehow still alive and put him out of his suffering (Keith is a hunter and outdoorsman). I dragged Yoda upstairs, tied him to his spot on his dog bed and fumed.

"Stay away from the dog!" I commanded to my sobbing kids.

I'd opted to forgo a kennel for the puppy, choosing to tie him in a special area in our living room with a dog bed, water, and toys always available instead if I couldn't supervise him. This way the boys could still chill out on the dog bed with him and I'd know he wasn't peeing in the house while I made dinner.

There Yoda was, on his dog bed, eyeing me.

"What did you do?" I yelled at him. Slowly, with building rage, I approached the adrenalin-filled killing machine I'd adopted, cared for, and loved for eight months.

That little puppy had fled the premises. In its place was a ball of rage watching another ball of rage approach.

Yoda curled back his lips as a snarl emanated from the depths of his being, and he lunged at me.

If he hadn't been tied down, this story would have ended much differently.

Keith came to the rescue again.

We'd begun some cautious chatting over our fences in the past weeks, and I was growing increasingly grateful for a friendly presence to turn to in a time I felt completely alone.

I was so far out of my normal range of functioning and thinking that I didn't even care that he was not just a hunter who hunted for meat— he was also a trapper who used traps to capture animals alive, so he could return to kill them and sell their fur.

Ordinarily I would recognize the enormous void between my beliefs and his and understand that issue was so huge to me, and to him as well, that it would be enough to keep us as nodding acquaintances at best.

But these were no ordinary times for either of us. He was spiraling out of control after a divorce and I had already spiraled way out there, so neither of us cared about our differences. We were just happy to have friendly chats over the fence.

That day, though, I took our conversation beyond the fence and called him.

"Can you come shoot this dog?"

I knew there was no way it was safe for us to keep Yoda. I'd called the rescue I got him from. They said at best they could have someone get him in a week, and they would put him down. No way was I going to have him in my home for one more night, let alone a week. I was too scared of him at that point to even get in the car with him.

Keith wasn't into the idea of putting a bullet in my dog's brain. Instead, he took Yoda to the vet, explained what had happened, and had him put down for me.

Now I'd managed to introduce three pets into our home, and they'd all died tragic deaths within weeks of each other.

I was on a roll.

But it gets better.

The powerful dog we'd brought into our family to protect us had turned on us. Literally, he'd turned on me. Whether or not his behavior was justified in the animal kingdom mattered not in my personal kingdom. We all felt betrayed again—and broken again.

My kids turned to me for comfort. All four of them piled every piece of their ever-breaking hearts onto my own broken shoulders, and as hard as I tried to bear the weight, it felt like too much to carry alone.

So I turned to Keith.

A year later we moved into a different house together.

Yup.

And before I get into that, let me round out the dog distractions segment in this portion of "How I added further complications and grief to our lives" with this:

I loved snuggling and spending time with the boys when they were little. I just did not have the energy to spend thirty minutes soothing each one individually as they went to bed, or enough arms to hold all four of them at once. This ate at me.

Now that we had a big, strong man in the house to protect us, I focused on the comfort aspect—how could I make sure none of the boys would lack a warm, loving presence when they needed one?

Puppies!

Yup. The guard dog thing had gone awry but now that we had the protection detail covered, how hard could it be to find a snuggly lovebug to grow and bond with each boy?

By now I had grown so bonded with my own dog Cassie that I felt guilty about the boys not having the love of a dog who looked at them as their primary person.

Never mind that they were still so young: Trevor was seven, Colin was six, Sean was five, and Jeremy was three. I decided Trevor and Colin were old enough for their own dogs, which would mean they always had that outlet of love on demand.

I promise you it made perfect sense at the time.

Keith had convinced me that a Treeing Feist would be the perfect dog for Trevor. They are small hunting dogs that climb trees to fetch squirrels. Seemed like a great idea even though I like big dogs and hate the idea of squirrel hunting.

So on a sojourn down south for a pretrial hearing, I brought my fellow widow, whose husband was killed with mine so we both made the trips for these hearings, and my friend Steve with me way out into the backwoods of North Carolina. Steve was friends with Lou and a JAG officer who was helping me through the trial. For a bunch of years during the trial and after, he remained one of my closest friends. There, down a long dirt road in the backwoods of North Carolina, was a trailer. In the yard surrounding that trailer were geese, and in a pen by the geese was a momma Treeing Feist with a litter of puppies around her.

I didn't give a moment's thought to the sanitary conditions (deplorable) or really much else. Instead, I selected a feisty little Feist, thanked the enormous dude who sold her to me, and laughed hysterically at my friends' faces as they watched me carry the puppy to them in the car while drop-kicking a goose that attacked me.

Just another day in my new normal.

Trevor scooped that puppy out of my arms, named her Luna, and remembered how to smile for real as he spent every moment with his very own dog. I took her to the vet who pronounced her healthy and gave her puppy shots—and two days later Luna was dead.

Yup. I brought my son a puppy to love and cherish after all the loss and heartache and confusion he'd endured. He held on to her just long enough to believe it was real and could safely love her, and wham! She became violently ill and died at the vet's office.

Parvo was the diagnosis, and the vet made no apology for declaring her perfectly healthy just a day before she became violently ill.

I was so completely off the rails at the time that I didn't even stop to challenge the vet or raise hell at what I still believe to be his incredible failure. All I knew was that I had to tell my son his puppy was dead too.

I mean, c'mon already, right?

Distractions have value, but not the kinds of distractions I was deploying. Every time I tried to avert the focus from pain, I seemed to shine a spotlight on new pain. You see, when I stopped moving for even a minute, the sheer terror of my life and enormity of my pain would literally render me useless. I would become so overwhelmed that the pain would escalate into proportions I could not endure. I had no clue how to help my boys when I couldn't even help myself. They— and I, I believed—were far better off keeping busy and focusing away from the pain because none of us knew how to cope with any of it.

So I would get them dogs, and take them on excursions, and find one distraction after another that only delayed pain or introduced more, rather than conquered it.

And I was nowhere near done yet.

If you can't be with the one you love, love the one you're with, right? No one explained to me that those are just words in a song, not a guidebook for grief.

While people around me either believed I was dishonoring Lou or had magically glued my heart back together, I got into a deeper relationship with Keith.

If I met him today, I may swap some fun conversation with him or develop a friendly acquaintance with him, and that's about it. He is a troubled soul but not a bad person. He is just completely, totally incompatible with the real version of me.

However, he was the seemingly perfect person for the broken, isolated, terrified, and desperate version of me.

You see, I truly believed still that I was not able to guide the boys on my own. I believed they needed a man not only to protect us all but to teach them how to be men.

I'd made one attempt before to equip them each with a male mentor now that their father was dead. Four Daddy Friends were selected by me from Lou's closest friends and family and were assigned to each boy. Their role was to spend regular time with each boy, one-on-one, to provide them with that bond with a male who also knew and loved their dad. In my mind, these guys would take my boys fishing, teach them how to play sports, show them how to shave, and do all those things dudes do for and with each other. But most importantly, and the driving force for this, they would also provide a steady supply of stories about Lou so the boys could get to know their dad in a different kind of way. It would be beautiful, in a sad way.

On a few occasions, on the same day, three of them showed up individually to take their assigned boy with them for a few hours out. Jeremy was too young for his assigned person's interest, so he stayed with me.

It occurred to me only in hindsight how it must have looked to neighbors who could see three dudes ring my doorbell and leave with a little boy, only to reverse the process a few hours later. I wonder how many of them thought I was the biggest whore on the block.

At any rate, all the Daddy Friends had kids of their own. Their wives and their sons expected them to be with them. One by one they phased out and that was that. Another swing, another miss. More upset in my kids' lives.

So I found them a man who would live with us and protect us, and who made me laugh and made me feel safe too—for a while.

The more difficult things became around me, the more arrows people shot into my heart, and the more I missed Lou, the more I turned to Keith to help me block it all out.

This, my friend, is a mistake. I do not recommend doing as I did in this instance.

There's at least one country song that talks about the healing to be found in loneliness. Those country artists know what they're singing about.

For a few months, I turned into that loneliness and found healing in it. Each night I sat outside watching the sky, talking to Lou, and talking to God—breathing and praying and thinking calmed me. It helped me find the strength to put one foot in front of the other each day and focus on my kids and on the trial.

I was building resiliency, but it was too little and too late.

Perhaps I would have managed to soldier on in strength if my husband had died in combat like normal people do in the military. Or even in an accident. Something that I could mentally have processed and not been forced to relive over and over for three-and-a-half years. But being murdered by a fellow soldier is not something I will ever truly be able to comprehend, and repeated trauma—in this case, three-and-a-half years of courtroom hearings and the trial, exposure to Lou's killer, and testimony about the murders—takes a massive toll on a soul.

There was all that, and there were other, personal issues related to family members that I will not fully divulge, as there are some things that should not be put out publicly. Trust me, it's been tempting given the ongoing impact it has on me, but that's as far as I'll go now. Let's just say that grief magnifies personalities and many a family has endured rifts as a result. In my case, a huge rift developed between my husband's family and me, and that was the extra weight that toppled me. Democrats and Republicans today probably have a better relationship than we did over the years.

Feeling abandoned by one family and afraid to burden the other, I felt completely alone and was physically so exhausted I would shake. I began drinking at night, with the kids in bed, and was often too drained to even cry. Other times I would turn the shower on high and hot and cry so much and so long the heat would almost make me pass out.

I was far from dishonoring Lou, and far from healed. I just didn't feel as if I should have to defend myself.

Conditions were ideal for Keith to assume a role in my life, and he did. It did not take long for me to recognize the huge mistake I'd made. Unfortunately, I was at least if not more stubborn than I was shattered, and I tried everything I could to deny that to myself. I would hold on to the sweet and fun moments as validation for the predominantly awful ones until finally, when I returned home after the acquittal, I cleared house.

Literally.

He moved out and I moved forward. My kids were again confused and most likely doubting my qualifications to raise them as much as I was.

Imagine if I'd chosen to reach out to a friend or a family member instead of attempting to carry this enormous load on my own. Imagine if I'd called my mom, who would have been over to my house in ten minutes and stayed as long as I needed her, instead of assuming she was too busy to help me. Imagine if I'd had a drop of self-confidence and believed in my own strength.

When you feel as if you are being stretched so much you are going to snap, it can feel impossible to withstand that pain. It can make you pray for death and it can make you do whatever you have to do to make the pain stop for even a moment.

Going through this myself has made me look at other people differently. I've stopped making snap judgments on what I see from the outside and I remember that what I see is just a sliver of that person's life. None of us can truly know what another person is living and enduring outside of our presence or behind social media.

I've learned that a bright smile can mask just as much pain as nasty behavior. I've learned that people who turn mean and cruel after trauma or tragedy most likely do not possess the grace or strength to behave otherwise, and I've learned how to separate myself from their behavior. I actually feel bad for them because I know what that untreated anger and pain do to a soul.

Flawless is absolutely not a word I would attach to myself, so that's not what I'm getting at here. I'm just exceedingly self-aware. Sometimes too much so, to the point of insecure, and I'm working on that. I've learned to recognize my breaking points and manage myself accordingly. I believe in apologizing sincerely and forgiving like I am often forgiven.

Too bad I had to keep sinking lower and lower before any of these lessons began to be learned. Maybe if I'd have had the opportunity to meet and learn from someone like Marie Cosgrove before I decided fleeing pain through distractions was a good idea, I'd have spared all of us some heartbreak.

Marie Cosgrove has been defying the odds from the very moment of her existence. Conceived from violence, born against doctors' advice, she was raised in a tumultuous blend of love and trauma, and was consistently told she'd never make it.

Even before she'd been born, doctors did everything they could first to convince Marie's mother, and then Marie's grandparents, not to give life to Marie.

A car accident had left Marie's mother with significant brain damage. Then she'd been raped and became pregnant with Marie. Doctors were certain that Marie would be born with major birth defects and insisted Marie's mother would not be able to care for such a baby—or any baby.

When Marie's mother refused the abortion, doctors went after Marie's grandparents to overrule their daughter. "She's not mentally competent," they said, and she should not have the baby.

The harder doctors fought to abort the baby, the firmer Marie's grandparents became, especially her grandmother. "That's why I'm here, because of my grandmother's faith and determination," Marie says.

Marie's grandparents assumed a large role in raising her. They loved her deeply and did their best to care for her. Some of her aunts and uncles loved her too, but the rest were cruel and even abusive. Her mother's moral compass was a casualty of her brain damage, which opened the door for Marie to experience horrific abuse during weekends in her mother's care.

All of her life she'd been told she was a blight on her family's name. She'd been physically abused and beaten. She'd been told she was worthless and should never have been born. In school she'd been told she was too dumb to go to college and no one would ever give her a scholarship anyway.

For a time she believed all the people who told her those things. She endured the abuse and the beatings because she felt she had no choice. Finally, she realized her kids were being abused as well. She immediately walked away from a career, her marriage, and her home to save her kids.

It was a tough time, but Marie was even tougher. No one, she vowed, would ever hurt her children again. She was going to do whatever it took to build a new life for herself and her kids, and nothing would stop her.

Marie is deeply embedded in the Christian faith. Her faith is what she turned to for the strength to overcome every obstacle placed in her path. When life gives her more than a lion's share of pain and cruelty, Marie roars right back at it with a might that seems impossible for her petite frame and unassuming demeanor.

Today Marie is a successful professional, having bought a company that once fired her. More than her professional success though, is the insight, inspiration, and resources she offers by teaching very hard-learned lessons from her life.

If you are a person of faith, Marie's voice will resonate with you. If you are not a person of faith, her message can also speak to you by showing you that the power of having something you believe in so strongly helps you find the strength and wisdom to persevere.

"All glory be to God," she says, "as I know this would not be possible if His guiding hand was not in my life. His guiding hand is in your life too if you simply allow Him in to show you how any mess you may be facing can become your message of triumph."

Maybe you are shouting Amen! at this. Or maybe you are rolling your eyes and thinking whatever. But whether Marie's faith in God touches you or not, her message of finding that source of power to turn your mess into a triumphant message of its own has merit.

I never went through the mad-at-God phase. It really never occurred to me to blame anything other than man's free will, including my own, for everything that happens in my life. For better or for worse. There is some gray area in that black and white, as far as good luck and bad luck, as well as people I believe God places in our lives. But mostly, it's on us to rise or fall to our potential.

If we are going to divert our energy and minds away from our pain, we should help ourselves out by diverting it to something positively powerful. For Marie it is her faith. What is it for you?

Chapter 5
On the Take

From the moment we learned Lou was killed, people from all over the country showed up to help in all sorts of ways. From the people who lined the streets to show support to the cards and letters I received to donations in a trust fund for the boys, hearts around the country opened up to us. I will never forget those people or those things, and I remain grateful for the strength they bestowed upon us all.

In time, more organized groups began reaching out to offer support. Over the years, one organization after another has popped up to support the families of the fallen. I am fortunate to have been a direct recipient of their kindness. I am also guilty of becoming dependent on that kindness.

It happens without you even realizing it, like any addiction. One person provides a moment of relief and another provides a moment of joy. When the high of those experiences wore off, or when the emergency relief fund ran out, I crashed until I could get my next fix.

Over time, I became so dependent on these events and these organizations that I stopped focusing on my own accountability for my happiness and independence. I transferred my dependence for happiness from Lou to them, in many senses. I pieced enough events together each year to ensure I'd attend one every few months. Some were with the boys and some were just for the widows, but they all offered their own splash of respite and recharging that was an absolutely critical part of my ability to get through several terrible years. Some of these organizations also stepped in to cover my bills when I reached the very bottom of the universe, just before I snapped back into fight mode.

I am indebted to these people and these organizations whose ripple effects still wash over me today.

The unfortunate, unforeseen, occasional impact of these organizations, though, is a culture of dependency and even reinforced victimhood and entitlement in many recipients.

There are different types of widows who attend and utilize these organizations. Most are able to use them sparingly without needing them. They graciously thank them for the support, attend an event, savor each moment, and return home to resume their own track of rebuilding their lives.

God bless them.

I was definitely not one of those women. I was instead the other type of widow—the one who counted the days until these gatherings, came alive when surrounded by my people, and crashed the moment I got home.

I was a professional widow. It was my identity. It was the first word I thought of when asked to describe myself. It was all I knew how to be. I was the victim, the broken woman who soaked up everyone telling me how strong I was and validating my pain for me.

When I got home and back into being the one everyone sought out to care for them, I instantly longed to be back among the people who took care of everything for me, who walked through parks with my kids and me, helped me laugh, and understood my tears.

I wanted to be back among the people who knew the enormity of my pain and with whom I could swap completely inappropriate widow jokes. It was as if I didn't fit in anywhere else than these insulated moments designed around our grief and where our husbands were hailed as heroes.

I didn't fit in, in my own world, where people complained about their husbands snoring, or wanting sex, or working long hours. I didn't belong all alone with my four boys at the Little League field for hours on end, carting all my kids to each other's seemingly endless games, surrounded by moms and dads doting on their own children and talking about family barbeques after the game. I didn't belong at either family's Christmas parties or weddings.

I didn't know where I belonged in the real world anymore and wanted to stay tucked in nice and safe with the people who got me.

I didn't realize how many of us had grown so completely dependent on these events until one organization grew to so many attendees it had to ask families who attended in the past to step back so new families could attend.

I was devastated at the thought that my kids and I would no longer be part of this extended family even as I understood the reality of the situation. The wars in Iraq and Afghanistan were not ending and casualties continued to climb. Wives were still being turned into widows on a regular basis and they, too, deserved this support, as did their children.

Within moments of receiving the email request, I opted my large family of five out of the next event—and cried my guts out.

When I hopped online to the widow groups shortly after, I was immediately bombarded with posts about other widows experiencing the same profound feeling of loss I was. We had all grown to believe this organization would always be a part of our lives, as it had for so many years running. With my boys it was the only event they cherished and looked forward to all year long, counting days for months sometimes, until it arrived. Telling them we would not attend that year was awful.

I watched their faces as they processed this loss. Tears were quelled before they had a chance to fall, and their little faces turned from crushed to resigned in seconds. Within moments of receiving the news, they'd absorbed the hurt, internalized it, and buried it beneath years of similar or stronger ambushes of pain.

I didn't know whether that was a good thing or a bad thing.

There is a fine line between accepting help and becoming dependent upon it. There is also a fine line between offering support and creating dependency.

Damned if you do, damned if you don't, if you're not careful.

For those organizations who offer support to any particular community—veterans, survivors, whatever—I highly recommend working with an advisory board composed of select people from within the community you serve. These people can talk like a peer to those who intentionally or unintentionally abuse the organization's generosity. They can provide you with enormous insight into the true needs of the community and offer unique comfort as well. Most organizations do this already, but for the ones that do not, I promise you it will be a game-changer.

There is another kind of professional military widow, and this is the one who not only holds herself back but also drains resources others could use. This is the woman who registers for every free trip, seminar, event, or item she can find. She flits around the country on other people's dimes as if it is her job—because it is, to her. She learns how to cry on cue and keep the tears in check when the situation calls for a more stoic widow. When she is in her free hotel room, she begins researching other events and applying to attend.

I realize this may sound harsh or even hypocritical of me, but the truth is there are people who for one reason or another—and I won't pretend to know their reasons—devote themselves to riding the widow train as long and as far as they can.

On the flip side, I've seen people and organizations exploit us and our families to fill their own needs. I've seen people pose as caring, patriotic Americans while around the cameras or in front of our families but know nothing about the women and children they profess to serve. I've seen top executives of nonprofits literally brush off some widows in a crowd as they rush to the side of a widow whose husband's death caught media attention and whose name is recognizable in the news.

The reality is there will always be people who exploit situations and people. Fortunately, there are even more people who do not.

Micah Fink is more than qualified to speak on the ins and outs of charitable support.

Micah is a former SEAL. His transition from service to civilian life was not an easy one. Struggling with the aftermath of combat and trauma, Micah didn't flee from that challenge so much as make a tactical retreat from it.

He headed straight for the jungle in Brazil. There he spent about six weeks on the river with an Indian guide, living off the land and staying in villages. "That was a big turning point in my life," he says. He rarely spoke. He hunted for his food in the midst of other predators. Jungle rot, mosquitos, and cougars became his new enemies, gradually diminishing the strength of the enemy within.

He jokes about that jungle journey, his smile flashing from beneath his beard, cowboy hat bobbing with his head as he laughs about the insanity of it all before shifting instantly back to his mission face and focus to explain how that experience changed things for him.

"I came back and really wasn't thinking much about my [combat] experiences. Was just thinking about that experience and it kind of became the new normal." That epiphany became the foundation upon which he's based his life ever since.

Struggle gives things value.

He knew that if that insight worked for him it could work for other veterans struggling against their own internal enemies. He also knew that the spas and drinking nights and fishing trips hold potential to be used as BAND-AIDs for symptoms of serious issues instead of meeting those issues at their root. That's what led him to launch Heroes and Horses, his foundation that utilizes hard-core survival and physical skills coupled with wild horses to help other veterans heal from their own traumas and build new foundations for their lives.

Veterans are warned that it's not a vacation. Those who make it through the rigorous selection process will not be pampered, wined, or dined. Rather, they will be pushed beyond their limits, spend days in the saddle and nights on the ground, live off the land, take meticulous care of their horses, and learn to look within themselves for the answers and strength they need to overcome the challenges before them.

The three-phased reintegration process of the Heroes and Horses program is intense, demanding, difficult, and beautiful. Its holy trinity of beliefs is:

1. People change only two ways: pressure and time.
2. It is purpose that allows you to overcome your external circumstances.
3. It's the struggle that gives things value.

This belief system is demonstrated to the veterans before even setting foot in Montana. The screening process is so thorough and specific that about 75% of applications are denied in at least one round of submissions. Micah isn't afraid to ask direct questions or dish out tough answers.

He doesn't pretend not to know that many applicants will be abusing some form of drug, and he doesn't disqualify anyone based on an addiction. He simply makes it clear that nonprescription drugs are not tolerated in this program, and he uses his intuition to seek out only those applicants he believes are committed to the process. Because while a prevailing component of the program is horses and their care, the program itself is not about making cowboys or horsemen—and it's not stingy with pressure.

By the time the third phase has been completed, veterans will have ridden 400 miles through stunning yet isolated land. They will have received intensive training in horsemanship and wilderness survival, and that training will be tested in extreme conditions. Finally, they will be matched with a wildlife outfitter far away from Heroes and Horses and will work for that company. This allows the veterans to experience the process of getting a job and getting back into the workplace. It can break a person, or it can change their life. The latter, says Micah, is what he has mostly seen happen.

At some point, each participant reaches the moment where they have to determine for themselves how to behave. Do they quit? Do they get mad? Or do they decide to take charge of their environment, to adapt to it, and use their own resources to mold that environment to them? It's a beautiful moment, Micah says, when you see that transformation take place. But they have to want it to happen enough to work for it, or the transformation will only be temporary.

Of all the programs and resources I've encountered, Micah's is the one that makes the most sense to me.

For men who are not veterans but also want to find the value in struggle and are willing to pay for that opportunity, Bedros Keuilian has your back. An Armenian refugee-turned-American entrepreneur, Bedros has an incredible story of tenacity and resilience. He also runs a different event for men that is built on the same foundation as Heroes and Horses, although the business model and the methods are different. He teams up with veterans like Ray Care and Steve Eckert to push men past their perceived limits to new potential. If you are a man or the parent of a boy, I highly recommend you check out Bedros Keuilian and The Project. I'll share more about Bedros and his work later.

For women, the closest thing I've found to The Project or Heroes and Horses is Robyn Benincasa's Project Athena.

Robyn is a San Diego firefighter, ten-time Ironman finisher, World Champion Adventure Racer, and three-time Guinness Endurance Paddling World Record holder. Her work with Project Athena pushes women of all fitness levels beyond their perceived limits during several day-long, arduous adventures packed with camaraderie and endurance. These are all women who are struggling to overcome their own setbacks, and ready to move into new happiness.

My recommendation for anyone seeking to immerse themself into resiliency, step outside comfort zones, build relationships, learn invaluable life skills and intense personal development—all of which result in emerging from the event not only with an entirely new perspective, but the confidence, drive, relationships, and clarity to apply toward achieving true potential—is to look these people up and learn about their programs to see if you are a fit. Or at minimum, find them online, read their books, watch their videos, and study their content.

Robyn's program is amazing. Still, there are other areas I'd like to see offered in events for women. So I designed my own event.

Train Your Pain pulls from the same well as the events I just shared, with my own spins. I incorporate self-defense, firearms training, and other tweaks into my program. As of this writing, New York is still under significant COVID restrictions. The moment this particular insanity ends, I will be opening the application process.

***

Here is something I like to do when I speak to groups of widows or other tragedy/trauma survivors:

I ask them to write ten words that describe themselves. The earlier they are into life after their loss the more likely the word widow tops their list. More often than not, words like broken, lost, and tired also appear on the list. This is understandable, especially for women in the first few years of life as a widow. But regardless of whether they are one month or ten years into their new normal, I always take time to help them reshape their lists.

Imagine if instead of describing yourself as "a broken, tired widow" or whatever words describe your pain and challenge like amputee, cancer patient, divorcée, you were able to redefine your own image of yourself.

Imagine if instead of writing only the terrible things about your life, you wrote only the good things like funny, fast, creative, blessed, loved, loving, talented, writer, animal lover, loyal.

Back when I could not find myself at peace anywhere other than surrounded by my fellow widows or among the waves of extraordinary volunteers who made us feel as if we were the only important thing to them at that moment, I would have written widow, victim, mom, mad, broken, tired, betrayed, sad, pain, and done.

Writing words on a piece of paper is not enough to make them be true. But by thinking it through and actively avoiding the words that focus on your pain, you deny those words power over you, if only temporarily. By writing words that you may have forgotten about yourself or buried beneath the grief and pain, you restore power to those words and reignite that part of your mind that believes them to be true. Whatever is watered will grow.

The same exercise can be used to have people think of their goals or dreams, and then have them list the things that have so far prevented them from achieving those things. This is an excellent way for me to understand the mindset of the people who entrust me with helping them overcome their challenges.

For instance, if I tell you my reason for not making a million dollars last year is because my husband is dead, I have four kids to raise on my own, my ex abused me and took all my money, and nobody is helping me or understands me, it is clear I am still mired in my pain without having reached the conclusion that I am responsible for my own path. Attempting to coach me professionally will require more personal development before moving into professional development. Think of a mortgage—for the first several years, your payments are mostly interest with very little of your principal being paid off. In time, that balance shifts as the principal is slowly paid down so the interest portion of the payment eventually matches the principal, and then swaps places in the balance of the loan.

If, however, I tell you my reason for not making a million dollars last year is because I failed at one business venture, have not figured out how to manage my time, am not sure what the next steps are, etc., it is clear I have separated my tragedy and trauma from my will to succeed and I am ready to talk business. Just like that mortgage payment with the principal paid down on which there will always be interest attached, the personal development part will remain a part of professional development, but not the primary focus.

Try this exercise for yourself, with this new perspective in place. If you find you are struggling to keep your list about anything other than your tragedy, trauma, or other loss, it's okay. Now you know where your first focus needs to be, before you can focus on moving forward professionally.

If you have someone in your own life who complains about being stuck, have them try this exercise, and help them understand themselves better too.

Chapter 6
Laugh and They Will Laugh with You

Humor is one of the most underutilized tools to overcome pain.

There's nothing like a good belly laugh to help you live in a moment. Babies and small children do this naturally. Once upon a time I did too, but I lost that for a while.

I did, however, escape into humor as often as possible. It didn't matter if there was nothing funny at all about a moment. In fact, the less funny a moment was, the more I felt like I needed to find something to laugh at. The choice for me was to laugh or cry. When I wasn't cracking a very poor taste joke about a very unfunny moment, I was feeling the pain of that moment in its full force, which was far too powerful for my unprepared soul to endure.

So I laughed at whatever I could.

I cracked jokes on the way to the funeral and cemetery. Then I sobbed and cried from the depths of my being. I had to be carried—literally—out of the wake when I dropped to the ground and begged to die after a phone call with someone who told me about Lou's conversation as he was dying.

Laughter can be healing. It can also be a deflection of feelings. It can be infectious, or it can be alienating. It can be extremely deceiving to both the person who is laughing and to those around them.

I have interviewed over 200 people as host of The American Snippets Podcast. Many of our guests have overcome major trauma or tragedy. I have interviewed people who fled Communist regimes, were tortured in Saddam Hussein's prison, were violently assaulted, lost someone they love to violence, suffered massive injuries in the line of duty, and others with their own incredible stories of resilience. All of them have moved past their pasts and into lives of further service and inspiration. They directly and indirectly inspire others and they create success where others see only failure. Most of these people have the best senses of humor around.

They crack jokes about things that are the opposite of funny but in which they extracted an excuse to laugh. They help others feel at ease by cracking jokes when a prosthetic ear falls off, or when sharing their stories. The laughter helps them reclaim a piece of victory.

One guest, Jason Schechterle, miraculously survived an explosion when the police cruiser he was driving was rear-ended. His burn injuries were catastrophic and left him very visibly disfigured. While he was in the hospital and no one knew if he would live or die, it became necessary to create a false name for him in order to give his family some peace from the media. His friends instantly came up with the alias Chris P.

Say that out loud and you will understand why that is so funny— or not funny, depending on your own sense of humor. (Chris P. = Crispy, in case you're struggling. You know, because he was burned to a crisp.) He cracked up when he told me that story, and he still uses that name for things like fantasy football.

Humor helped Jason and those who love him through those times. Humor still helps him.

Looking back, I realize I used laughter as a deflection. Those around me who were also hurting deeply were all too glad to join in and crack their own jokes as well. Those who were tasked with managing me learned it was easier to just give in and roll with me. Those who did not know me thought I was an asshole.

At least the jurors, called panel members in the military, did. Some of them anyway.

The prosecutors may have been taken aback by the dark jokes and the attempts to smile, but they quickly learned it served a purpose in tense family meetings and seemed relieved to be offered this assist.

I think.

Two judges oversaw the court martial. Colonel Parrish was first, and Colonel Stephen Henley later appointed himself to ensure the trial tanked, based on his rulings. Neither of them was amused by me.

WHAT NOT TO WEAR TO A MURDER TRIAL

To be fair, I'm not sure either of them truly possesses a soul, so perhaps they find no amusement at all in anything that does not feed their power. (Yes, I know this all seems very bitter of me but if you've read my book, Front Toward Enemy, I daresay you agree.)

Some of the panel members really didn't like me. And that's not just paranoia talking. I probably wouldn't have liked this version of me either if I were them.

From their vantage point, sitting in that courtroom and looking at me seated with the other family members in attendance, they saw the woman who is supposed to be a grieving widow with an almost constant smirk on her face. If they cared to watch me instead of the witnesses—and based on conversations I was later told about, it seems as if the witness testimony meant little to them, as their minds were made up well before the trial ended—they would see the supposedly grieving widow scribbling notes on her pad, sharing them with her seatmates, and choking back laughs. They would see my upper body bouncing as my legs beneath me popped up and down, up and down, for hours. And probably the worst moment of all happened in the bathroom.

Our families were kept strictly away from the defendant and the panel members, except in the bathrooms. My father-in-law came face-to-face with Lou's killer at the bathroom sink one day.

Me? I had no idea one of the crankiest panel members of all was in the bathroom while my mother-in-law and I were in the stalls.

It was another intensely brutal day of testimony. Every moment of the whole experience drained the life force right out of us, it seemed. So in a rare moment of lightness between my mother-in-law and me, I bantered with her that, "The family that pees together, gets to watch an execution together," or something equally unfunny.

We exited the stalls snickering with execution jokes on our lips, only to see Major Carmela Crespo standing almost at attention near the sink. This panel member had already shot us—me, anyway—one disapproving look after another during proceedings, and I knew this moment was not going to help. Worse, she was married to another panel member—yes, that's right, Colonel Henley sat two married people on the same panel, both of whom expressed a clear stance of doing whatever it took to not sentence a person to death, because they are so strongly opposed to the death penalty that even if their own son were to be murdered, they would not support the death penalty for his killer.

Sigh. I digress.

Major Carmela Crespo's husband had been nicknamed Captain Angry by us because he looked like he was constantly pissed about something.

That was the moment I realized that I needed to dial myself down a bit.

Unfortunately, as far as some panel members and the judges were concerned, I'd sealed my fate. I know personal feelings aren't supposed to play a part in decisions or thought processes in a court martial, but I'm convinced some of the panel members found it even easier to acquit the man they knew to be guilty, or simply not care about it at all, because they had no respect for me. Respect, in the military, is everything. And to at least two female panel members, panel forewoman Colonel Fiorey and Major Crespo, it was clear to see I disgusted them. I don't believe they based their acquittal on my behavior. I just think I made it easier for them to behave the way they did in the deliberations.

If they only knew, I thought. If they only knew I didn't mean any of the jokes or disrespect, I just couldn't absorb the enormity of the constant onslaught of trauma and pain being hurled at us as we endured the three-and-a-half-year process. If only they saw me the moment I was back in the apartment where I stayed for the trial, unable to sleep, crying for hours, and completely lost.

This is one of the many areas we, especially me apparently, could have benefitted from counseling and support services during the judicial process. In the next chapter I share another incident that rams this home so I won't go deep here, but any trained professional would have recognized the signals all of us sent out that our pain was crushing us, and they could have alleviated some of that for us with therapy or counseling. My husband was one of two victims in this case, and both families of both victims were in attendance. Both families were wracked with pain, and we all showed obvious signs.

For me it was the absurd behavior sprinkled with angry outbursts or rounds of tears. For some it was all anger all the time; for others it was either a steadfast stoicism only occasionally breached with tears, but usually with anger, or a total submersion into the role of victim, comparing their grief to others' and declaring themselves the most aggrieved of all.

It was a freaking circus, and trauma was the ringmaster.

I still crack jokes about moments that are stressful. In fact, I have developed my own measurement of a situation's severity by determining how long it will be before something stressful turns into a funny memory. For instance: the septic tank backing up, filling the house with nauseating stench, requiring me to dig up the lid under frozen ground, and costing thousands of dollars to replace. I knew it would take many months before that memory made me laugh. But even as my son and I battled the frozen earth and hated every second of it, I was able to keep us both in the game by talking through the timeline before it would be funny. That perspective—reminding ourselves that in the big picture of life this was just a nanosecond of stress—helped.

Other moments become funnier more quickly.

A couple years ago I was doing my best to spruce up an area of our basement. My oldest son was coming home to visit and decided he'd rather sleep down there than share with his brother upstairs. Privacy outweighed aesthetics.

To make it seem less like a basement, I set to work putting soft tiles on the floor, stringing lights, setting up a bed and a sitting area, and hanging curtains for privacy. Beyond the range of the soft tiles, I hummed to myself while I fastened sheer curtains to the ceiling, so the stacks of bins against the wall would be concealed. I was excited and happy and hurrying to hang the last curtain before my sisters arrived for some cocktails in the sun.

"Haste makes waste," my grandma used to say.

She was right.

In my own haste, I somehow believed I could use cardboard boxes that held inflatable water tubes as a makeshift stepping stool. Piling three boxes up, I scrambled to the top box and hurried to tack that last curtain up.

Because physics didn't give a shit about my day or my happiness, the cardboard predictably crumbled and I came crashing down onto the concrete floor.

I knew instantly that I'd just broken my arm. The pain was familiar from the other times I'd broken my arms. I knew I had just created about five or six more weeks of healing and a few months of rehabbing my arm because I constantly injured it.

I was not happy, and yet, as I managed my breathing to get a handle on the pain, I was also smiling.

I knew my sisters would be there any minute and make me go to the emergency room. I also knew they would find it hilarious, and I was about to be mercilessly mocked— deservedly so—for my stupidity. I knew that it was already funny, even though it sucked. I started laughing at the ridiculousness before I even stood up.

Just like that, a stressful situation became less stressful. My mindset shifted away from "Poor me," and toward "Let's take care of this and forge onward."

I swallowed the urge to vomit, made sure I wasn't crying, and walked outside to soak up some sun.

Maybe, I thought, I could pretend nothing was wrong long enough to have at least one drink and relax before I spent the rest of a sunny day in the ER. But since I had to hold my dead right arm up with my left, my sisters caught on quickly. They did indeed enjoy some hearty laughs as they drove me to the ER.

Almost a year to that day I launched off my son's Boosted Board and cracked my arm again. Some of us will do anything for a laugh.

***

The next time you are faced with a stressful situation, pause a moment. Imagine sitting around with friends, swapping stories. Imagine telling the story of what is happening right now. Is there a joke in there somewhere? Is there something so completely opposite of funny that it's funny? Is there a lesson in there somewhere that holds something funny in it? (Which reminds me, when teaching your young children to do their own laundry, never leave a bottle of bubble bath on top of the washing machine!)

I know so many people who come completely undone at any level of stressful moment. Why? Because they don't find any humor in the moment.

Yes, I am all too aware that a great many moments are devoid of humor or the potential for humor. But isn't that all the more reason to make sure we don't miss out on the moments that do have humor, or which at least hold potential for future humor?

Think of all the 2020 jokes going around. There's not much funny about any of it, is there? But something about a meme makes pretty much anything funny to someone.

If we can all find something humorous about any of the insanity sweeping our country, why can't we find the humor in a flat tire or getting dumped or being constipated or accidentally pissing someone off or breaking a nail or being stuck in line or any of the routine things that irritate us so much?

Chapter 7

What Not to Wear to a Murder Trial, and Other Advice for Navigating Traumatic Loss and the Criminal Justice System

While this chapter does zero in on advice for crime victims or survivors of crime victims, don't skip it just because nothing like that has ever happened to you or someone you love. First—and try not to let this freak you out—none of us can absolutely guarantee we won't be victimized or survivors or family members of a victim or victims. I don't care who you are: evil exists and, while it can be dissuaded, it cannot or will not always be prevented.

Next, this chapter is not all about murder.

It makes me want to vomit every time another news story pops up with someone saying, "Things like this happen to other people," or "in other towns."

If you really believe that, you need a hefty dose of reality to prepare yourself before "things like this" happen to someone you know. Someone you love will die one day. God willing, not via tragedy or violence, but they will die. And you can bet your box of tissues and all the Xanax in the world that you are better off acknowledging that this will happen. You're better with the mindset that you may be crippled with pain when it does, but that you will train that pain before it trains you. Swaddling yourself in the illusion that bad things only happen to other people in other places or in the news instead of to you or someone you love is just plain naïve and maybe even narcissistic.

I recommend you read Jason Redman's book, Overcome, after you read this one. Jason, by the way, is a former Navy SEAL who got shot in the face. He also went through and overcame major personal and professional crashes outside of those injuries, so his book makes my tough love look like Mary freaking Poppins is singing to you.

WHAT NOT TO WEAR TO A MURDER TRIAL

There is a lot of advice I wish I'd been given to help me navigate the immense trauma of the murder trial. One thing I wish I'd had help with was understanding what to wear.

I know this seems like an incredibly trite thing to say after all that bluster I just blew at you. But hear me out because this lesson really would have helped me, and it may help you one day.

Here's the backdrop to the lesson:

The judicial proceedings we were rolled up in were in the military courts. The military has strict uniform regulations and a certain code of respect as a rule. Although our judge, Colonel Henley, told the panel to be comfortable and excused them from the odious task of wearing their properly respectful Class A uniforms to the proceedings, this did not mean the panel members dropped their own beliefs on what proper attire meant. They may have enjoyed wearing their comfy BDUs (the former camouflage uniform known as the Battle Dress Uniform), but still, they had standards and definitely judged others by appearance, apparently more than they judged the Accused by the evidence, but I digress.

So you have members of the military, long trained to be meticulous about their attire and to dress respectfully, and who held others to the same standard ... and then you had me.

I suck at being a girl. Always have. I've never known how to do my hair, or put makeup on, or what to wear anywhere. When I was a kid, I used to have to put skirts and dress shoes on for church and I was the only girl in my class who wore skirts to school every day because of the household rule that we had to dress up. My wardrobe consisted of whatever my three older sisters wore before me. I have zero natural fashion sense and my wardrobe at the time of the trial was largely jeans and sweatpants. That was strike #1 against me.

Next, time was not my friend. If I slept two-to-three hours a night that was a lot. The rest of the time I was unfortunately awake and my traumatized soul was in constant torment. The day I was finally supposed to speak for Lou, even if for only a moment, was no different. I did a decent job of putting on a business dress that day and keeping my hair kind of okay. My plain black pumps were a problem though. One of them broke and the only other pair of shoes I had was a pair of stiletto-type heels with crisscross straps. I threw a long sweater on top of the just-above-the-knee dress and all was well, except for the fact that my testimony was pushed to the next day.

That threw me into a complete jumble. I'd saved that dress for that occasion and couldn't wear it twice in a row, I thought. The emotional turmoil of mentally preparing myself to take the stand for just those few moments had been intense. By the end of the day, the level of emotion and stress I experienced was off the charts, and by two a.m. I gave up on sleep entirely.

I did my best to kill time by running a few miles on the treadmill, but that still left me several hours before court that day.

My parents had brought my kids down to Fort Bragg to visit me, and they were all sound asleep in the apartment. After I boiled myself in the shower and air-dried my hair, I still had a couple hours of forced stillness, while inside I was screaming.

My solution was to drag out a set of hot rollers, blow the dust off the top, and drink the first pot of coffee while I rolled my hair for the first time … ever, maybe. I don't even remember when I got those rollers or why I brought them there but there they were, and I zoned out while taking as long as I could to roll every single one into my head.

I could feel my scalp burning and smell my hair joining suit, but it didn't faze me. The smell of burnt hair and broken dreams blended with coffee seemed the perfect accessory for my mood and my life.

Eventually I unrolled the rollers and my hair exploded all around my head. The clock ticked a little closer to wake-up time for the normal people in the world and I turned my attention to what to wear as I started in on another pot of coffee.

I was pissed at everyone and everything, especially at the judge for continuing to make this process as awful as it could possibly be, and then doubling that. I was pissed that the media was less interested in the proceedings than we needed it to be—no one was babysitting this process, and it was easy to see it was completely unraveling with impunity. Rulings this judge made were outrageous. I describe them in my first book, Front Toward Enemy. When I would tell anyone with any legal knowledge about these rulings, they would say I must be mistaken because no judge would do that.

Ha.

But there I go, digressing again.

My mind flashed back to the first days after Lou was murdered. I'd been besieged by the media then, and completely disinterested in accommodating them. Finally I'd relented, telling Frank, my military-appointed babysitter known as a Casualty Assistance Officer, to just have them all come at once so we can do this one time and be done with it.

I had no idea I'd just called a press conference, but all the networks did, and they all showed up.

In honor of being on every news station in the country that day, I put one of Lou's 101st Cavalry t-shirts on, matched it with a baggy pair of shorts, wiped the snot off my face and marched out on my front lawn. My kids looked pretty much the same.

Frank advised me after that: "Barb, if you want people to care about this and follow it, you have to make them like you. Maybe dress nicely."

Three-and-a-half years later, in the bedroom of my Fort Bragg apartment, hours before I would finally get to bring Lou's name and memory into these proceedings, those words came back to me.

There were some faithful reps from big papers attending most days and very often a local news crew would show up with a camera for a comment. So on that day, I thought, I would not let them see me broken. I would not let them see me as dismissible or weak. I would dress up as if I were meeting Lou, and his jaw would drop at my beauty.

A black pencil skirt hugged my hips and offered a nice contrast to the snug, red, just-off-the-shoulder sweater with a cowl neck I assumed offered an innocent and respectful tone to my getup. I even put pantyhose on for the occasion and slipped my size 8 ½ bricks into those black crisscross strap stiletto heels to complete the look.

"Mom, why are you trying to look like a girl today ... are you going somewhere again?" asked my six-year-old son as I walked out of the bedroom. The question was funny because he was totally serious. They'd learned that the only time I wore anything but shorts, jeans, or sweatpants was when I was leaving.

I did the best I could to keep it light. "Yeah bud, I have to go to the trial again today, remember?"

His little-boy face, big cheeks, crazy hair, and deep hazel eyes just like his dad's all seemed to fall at the same time as my son dropped his chin to his chest before looking back up at me and shaking his head sadly. "Mom," he said, his voice breaking with emotion and pity, "I feel so bad for you."

My heart immediately pounded harder as I processed my little boy's pain and incredible empathy for what I was going through, until he completed his thought. "I know it's so hard for you to look like a girl and you have to do it every day here!"

I didn't give my appearance another thought until it was way too late to realize the error of my ways.

Alone in the witness room, I paced back and forth awaiting the guard to come fetch me. When he did, I was over-eager to say my husband's name in court—to make them all hear about the victim who was rarely mentioned throughout this trial as if he didn't matter at all. I wanted to scream everything about him that I loved, so that they would all know him and think of him throughout the process. In reality I knew I was only going to have a moment on the stand, to identify a picture of Lou as my husband and confirm I knew he was dead. This was the beginning of the guilt or innocence phase, not sentencing, so telling Lou's true impact would have to wait.

Still, I was a mess of nausea, fatigue, and hair spray as I entered the courtroom and immediately recognized what an idiot I was.

Colonel Henley was the first one to quietly judge me with raised eyebrows and an outright little smirk as he cautioned me to be careful not to trip on the slew of wires running pell-mell across the floor.

Doing my best to quash the insecurity that had tripled in my gut, I made another mistake of looking ahead of me, directly into the eyes of Major Carmela Crespo, the member who would later bump into me in the bathroom.

Major Crespo could not, or maybe just would not, control her disdain for me by literally rolling her eyes and shaking her head, crossing her arms in front of her chest and hitching one leg over the other as if to barricade herself from the scene before her. Colonel Fiorey, the forewoman, also shook her head openly at me while several of the other members smiled like someone would at a child who said something amusing.

It was a disaster, and I knew I'd lost their respect before I ever had a chance to earn it. It was that palpable. Even our team of prosecutors looked bemused by my mistakenly selected Lifetime movie widow outfit.

I know I didn't simply imagine these reactions because later on, a Criminal Investigations (CID) Special Agent confirmed to me that several of the guards began to talk about things they'd like to do with me outside of the courtroom after that.

Maybe once upon a time I would have found that flattering. In this case I found it horrifying.

That moment is burned into my brain. I just didn't carry the lesson it held until I'd had time to reflect.

That day in the courtroom, as I left the witness stand and returned to my front-row seat, all I could think was that I'd just epically failed Lou. The disdain the panel held for me would bleed over into their indifference to him, and he would be further forgotten.

This wardrobe disaster was not to blame for the outcome of the trial, but it definitely contributed to my discomfort and challenged the panel's ability to sympathize with me—and we needed them to care about us and our husbands and all the pain because it was becoming evident that we were at risk of seeing a killer acquitted.

Anyone who finds themself tangled up in a criminal justice trial, whether as a victim or survivor of a victim, needs to remember that appearance does matter and judgment does take place before the trial ends. Regardless of juror instructions, there is simply no way to remove 100% of human subjective thoughts. Even if those panel members actively told themselves not to factor in any disdain for me, which I can pretty much guarantee at least three of them made no such effort, their subconscious minds would already be holding on to that impression.

The bathroom incident I shared earlier occurred after this day in court. Major Crespo, already inclined to dislike me, now padded that inclination with this experience. Bit by bit those moments and impressions added up. That her husband sat on the panel with her was doubly damaging, because there is no way I will ever believe those two did not discuss any aspects of this case—especially those not related to testimony—between themselves.

There is no reason any victim or survivor should ever cross paths with jurors or the Accused in the courthouse. Unfortunately, there is also not much to be done to prevent that from happening. Violent crime is traumatizing. Surviving it, or surviving a victim of it, is traumatizing. If you find yourself in this situation, it is going to test every drop of your strength and faith to overcome it. Do not rely on those within the criminal justice system to shield you from unexpected encounters, or to think to coach you on appearance or demeanor. Maybe they will and all will be well in those areas, but maybe they won't, and you will potentially experience similar moments as I did. Do not be afraid to ask for guidance on attire, escorts into public bathrooms, or information on the culture into which you are a guest, because that's what you will be in the courtroom—a guest.

You are entering the domain and world of the judge, the attorneys, the bailiffs, the court reporters, and even the jury, who will be feeling more a part of the culture than you likely will. Alienating any of them may not directly impact the outcome of the trial but it will cause greater discomfort and stress than you are already experiencing.

While earning my master's in criminal justice, I wrote my thesis titled "Murder in the Military." Coincidentally, the capital court martial of another soldier accused of murdering two of his superior officers while in a combat zone was taking place at the same time. I left my kids with my boyfriend at the time, something I still regret, to spend over two months in Georgia so I could witness that trial, compare it to ours, and learn more about how it all works. Plus, I still had an unhealthy addiction to violent crime cases.

It was in that courtroom, as I sat alone in the back, respectful of the victims' families, that a young JAG officer slid into the bench next to me.

"You're Barbara Allen, aren't you?"

At first I was annoyed. I thought I was about to be kicked out of the courtroom. It was still early in the trial and no one knew who I was or why I was there. Most of them thought I was a reporter.

"Yes," I answered warily.

"I read your book!" were his next words. I could not have been more surprised as he continued, telling me that reading my book not only shocked him from a legal sense but also opened his eyes to the plight of victims and their survivors. Because of my book, he said, he would move forward with extra consideration for the families. He would never dismiss them or forget their rights to understand their cases, etc.

If nothing else ever came of me writing Front Toward Enemy, that alone would have justified everything I put into it.

Attending that court martial also made it clear that there is enormous disparity between how cases are handled and how victims are treated, depending on where it happens and who is involved.

The criminal justice system is not uniform. Neither is the Uniform Code of Military Justice. Laws are often interpreted subjectively, and politics absolutely come into play. In the Bozicevich case, the prosecution team remained intact, while ours had more shift changes than McDonalds. The judge showed impartiality, refusing to allow either side to step outside the lines of the law. The victims' families were kept fully informed without having to demand information, and the government expert working the case was relentless in his commitment to justice.

This case was the only time I experienced the criminal justice system work the way it's supposed to. The defendant was found guilty and sentenced to life in prison.

Everything about that case, from professionalism in and out of the courtroom to the verdict, was the polar opposite of our case.

If you ever find yourself in the difficult position of being involved in a criminal trial as a result of violent crime done to yourself or someone you love, you need to understand that justice has less to do with the truth and everything to do with what happens in the courtroom—what evidence is dismissed and what is permitted, what either attorney knows about a witness that can be used to place pressure on that witness or otherwise distort their credibility or testimony, how the jury is picked and who they are.

My friend Taya Kyle is someone who can unpack all of this with me any time I feel the need and vice versa. Her husband Chris and his best friend Chad Littlefield were murdered by the veteran they were donating their time and experience to support.

Taya, already in the spotlight due to her husband's fame as The American Sniper, found that spotlight to be magnified after her husband's murder. She has never really had the opportunity to face any significant challenge, no matter how personal or how painful, without the glare of that spotlight.

She, too, experienced the hostile environment of a murder trial and the helplessness of watching the case unfold. The verdict in that case should have signified the beginning and the end of her legal troubles. Unfortunately, she has repeatedly been pulled into emotionally draining lawsuits.

There were other people and other issues that were extremely painful and shocking, but betrayal and fame seekers seem to be part of the "norm" in her world. The people who kicked her while she was down don't warrant mentioning by name. I only mention them at all because it's important to note the layers of pain she navigated and continues to navigate today. That she does so and still gives so much of herself is extraordinary. She had to walk through all of this in the very public spotlight while navigating her grief, leading her children through theirs, and experiencing the might of the keyboard warrior army, comprised of bitter, unfulfilled people pronouncing judgment on her based on none of the facts.

In spite of all she went through, Taya persevered through her pain. She's achieved significant success, inspired countless people (including me), and impacted even more lives through the nonprofit she launched. Check out the Chris and Taya Kyle Foundation to see for yourself.

We've swapped endless anecdotes and insight gleaned from these combined experiences. She, too, understands the futility of seeking any sort of control over outcomes she is powerless about. She, too, experienced the insult of being judged by appearance and she, too, knows the power of digging deep into your faith and humor to access strength.

WHAT NOT TO WEAR TO A MURDER TRIAL

You are essentially powerless in terms of how the case is handled, so you must learn to separate your well-being from the progress and outcome of the case.

That is much easier said than done. Believe me, I know. But just as with any other life event, attaching your sense of power or happiness to an outcome you have no control over is setting yourself up for disaster.

How big of a disaster is proportionate to how much of your happiness you have attached to an event.

For instance:

"My wedding will be perfect if the sun is shining."
"My career will take off if I get this promotion or nail that meeting."
"If anything happens to my brand-new car, I will be so mad!"
"If my husband dies in Iraq, my life is over too."
"If the killer is acquitted, I will never recover."

I could go on, but you get the point.

Bad weather on your wedding day may not be what you wish for, but it doesn't have to diminish your joy one bit. The week before I married Lou it was sunny and warm. The day I married him it was freezing and we had snow flurries. I still loved every minute of that day.

If you don't get that promotion or you make a mess of that meeting, it does not mean your career is over. It just means you have to keep trying.

A ding in your new car? Or a smashed bumper, or even total destruction? Ha. I've been there and done that too many times to count, from my own very first piece of crap car I wrapped around a tree the day after I spent every last penny I had on it to having teenage boys do everything from scratch to total my vehicles. Is it stressful? Yup. But I've always been grateful that no one was injured in any of the accidents.

I know I talked about mindset earlier, but I warned you I would repeat some things that are especially important. You already know that I programmed myself to self-destruct if tragedy struck, well before the strike occurred. Three-and-a-half years was apparently not enough time for me to have recognized the error of my ways there because I did the exact same thing with the trial.

I repeated the same mistake of attaching my well-being to the outcome of the trial, and I suffered the same consequence.

All along I told myself I was living to see Lou's killer die. Then I convinced myself as long as he was found guilty, I would be okay, even if he was just sentenced to life in prison. I could no more imagine watching Lou's killer go free than I could have imagined the military appearing at my door to tell me Lou was dead. I could not fathom the possibility that I would have to live knowing the killer got away with it. It was simply too enormous a loss to consider and my brain would not allow me to do so.

Instead, I focused on revenge. I focused on taking some measure of joy knowing Lou's killer would suffer for the rest of his life. I focused on some restoration of fairness in the world when the killer was held accountable and justice was met.

And I paid dearly for that.

Sometimes it is still hard to process the enormity of everything I've gone through. Plenty of people experience the impact of violent crime, but very few are emotionally prepared for it when it happens to them or someone they love. The lessons this taught me personally, as well as the insight I've gained from getting to know and learn from others who have gone through major trauma, are serving me well in everyday life. They can serve you too.

Here are some of those lessons discussed above, in a tidy list:

- The time to acknowledge the inevitability of loss in your life is now, so you can build a resilient mindset before you need it most.
- Appearance does matter. In and out of a courtroom, make sure you understand the culture you are entering and treat it with respect. There is a difference between asserting your uniqueness and disrespecting a culture.

- Do not rely on anyone to protect or shield you from offensive, harmful, or traumatizing moments or exposures. It's great to have a safety network and people looking out for you, but at the end of the day there are no guarantees they will succeed.
- Do not be afraid to ask for guidance/help.
- Never attach your own sense of well-being to an outcome you cannot control.

Chapter 8
Fight

I talked about the flight defense mechanism in chapter four. Now it's time to look at the fight response.

None of us can know for sure how we will respond in times of danger. Will we run into a burning building to save someone, or will we run away? Will our brain's flight response outpower our fight?

We experience this conflict on an almost daily basis. Most of us just aren't aware of it. Our brain's function is to keep us safe. This means it works to maintain smooth functioning in all systems, rushing to shut down anything that invades or threatens that inner peace. Snooze buttons, for instance, are an excellent example.

Your brain knows you are comfortable in bed. It knows that getting up requires you to push past discomfort, and that you'd be much happier going back to sleep. It encourages you not to leave your comfortable safe space and upset your system. You are engaged in a battle between fight or flight before you've even opened your eyes. Fight through your hangover or aching back or dread of the day before you, or whatever else you'd rather not face, to get out of bed and begin your day—or flee from all of that and delay it all by staying in bed for ten more minutes.

Your decision there sets the tone for the rest of your day even if you don't know it.

Ever since I met Bedros Keuilian, I cannot hear my alarm go off without hearing him tell me, "Get up, and don't be a bitch!" Maybe that's offensive to you. Maybe that is not your cup of tea and you cannot understand why I support that or respond to it.

To each his own, and for me there is a time to be soft and a time to open up a can of whoop-ass. Most of the time I level-up harder for a challenge than I do for cajoling. But that's just me. At any rate, whether you roll that way or not, Bedros has the story to back up his tough love, and love is the place all he does comes from.

Born in Communist Armenia, Bedros has vivid memories of life without any of the things Americans take for granted, things like grocery shelves that are fully stocked and limitless potential in a capitalist economy.

Necessity breeds one of two things: despair or grit. While the Keuilian family may have experienced despair, they never let it outmatch their grit. Whether it was diving into dumpsters, siphoning gasoline to use for head lice treatment, or risking everything to escape Armenia—where there was a need, they dug deep and pushed through challenges until they found a way to solve that problem.

"Anyone who's gone down some path of bankruptcy, of divorce, of disease, near death, crime, whatever it is, you can bounce back. But you have to make the choice to not be a victim and be the victor," he says.

Bedros openly talks about the anger inside of him that began to grow into a dominant force in his life.

The anger began in Armenia when he was four years old. For two years, he suffered repeated sexual abuse in silence. His abusers stayed in Armenia, but the confusion and anger traveled with him to America. Then came the bullying and callousness from people in the land they'd gone through so much to arrive in.

"Go home, foreigner!" or "Go back to your fucking country!" is what Bedros heard more often than anything else. He eased into adolescence and puberty as an overweight and insecure boy on the outside, with a simmering feeling of resentment on the inside.

The anger grew until he could no longer contain it, and it seeped out through violence. Carjacking, home invasions, robberies—Bedros did all of those. "Don't ever try to outrun a police helicopter," he advises with a laugh. "I was one of those idiots who tried that and failed."

Fitness and physical training is the path that led Bedros out of anger and into fulfillment.

A high school classmate led Bedros into the physical fitness world and it was there, while he was pushing himself, that the burning muscles tamed some of his burning anger. It was there that he changed his outward appearance and began to feel better about himself. Fitness became his new outlet for his energy, and he pursued it after high school.

Today Bedros is in command of an eight-figure empire. Fit Body Bootcamp is his international personal training franchise and Empire Systems is his high-level business coaching company. Bedros runs a mastermind with another king in the health and fitness industry, Craig Ballantyne, and he speaks at selective events and is absolutely committed to using his **personal success** to give back in various ways.

Children's charities are at the top of Bedros's charitable focus. Bedros and his wife have unofficially adopted more than ninety children through Compassion International and are dedicated contributors to Shriners Hospitals for Children. They've also donated close to $500,000 to Toys for Tots. With each dollar he donates, says Bedros, "another piece of the child inside me heals."

He fights the memories of his past by protecting the futures of others.

Bedros also runs The Project, an exclusive, three-day immersive experience for men designed to help them find their inner beast and maximize fulfillment in their fitness levels, their finances, and their families.

Once you know all that about him, does that change your reaction to his "Don't be a bitch!" when the snooze button goes off?

The whole snooze button thing is about more than just catching extra sleep or jumping into your day. Either you are going to take the lead on your day and attack your challenges, or your challenges will take the lead and dictate your day. Hitting the snooze button programs your brain to be a little bitch that day. It sets you up to not feel confident and to not do that thing you've been wanting to do. It sets you up to put half the effort into your relationships, your workout, your big meeting—all of it.

But if you pop up when the alarm sounds, you are telling yourself that you are going to dominate the day. You are telling yourself that you will push past discomfort, do that thing you've been avoiding doing, and do it on your terms. Instead of running behind and getting to work late or barely on time, you'll be on time or early.

Is it possible for a snoozer to switch gears and seize their day? Is it possible a pop-upper will switch gears and have a mediocre day?

Of course. But the snoozer will have to work harder than they would have to get out of the mindset they placed themself in and into another. The pop-upper will have an easier time catching themself in their slip and getting out of the snoozer mindset.

Someone who is genuinely invested in their day, with the mindset that they are blessed to be alive and the confidence that they will outperform their pain points today, is less likely to hit that snooze button. They are more inclined to attack their challenges instead of run from them.

I know this and other invaluable techniques to train my pain not only from interviewing people like Bedros, but from my own experience.

For years, I lost my ability to recognize there was still a fighter inside of me. Not that there weren't occasions that I glimpsed a fighting spirit, it's just that that spirit was more like a drunken fighting spirit, full of bravado and poorly executed thoughts. But then there were moments when the fight instinct barged forth in surprising fury.

It was a spectacular spring day in New York, and I had the windows wide open all over the house. Music playing on my phone wafted in between the water as I showered. Suddenly the tunes skipped a beat, and then another, at the precise moment my dogs began barking their heads off outside. Don't you love getting phone calls when you're in the shower?

I realize more people let the phone just ring and see who called after their shower. But since I still struggle with missing Lou's last call, I rarely ignore a ringing phone, even if to just check and see if it's someone I love.

Grumbling in irritation, I wrapped a towel around my drenched body and answered the phone in one move.

It was hard to hear what was being said on the other end. With a poor connection and a four-dog chorus outside the window, I barely made out the voice of the reporter scheduled to come interview me the following day.

"Yes," I said, as I assumed she was asking me if we were still on for the next day. "I'm cleaning my house today so it will be ready for you tomorrow."

It had been a while since I'd done any kind of news interview. When Lou died and it became known he was murdered by another soldier,

I'd been bombarded with media calls. Sporadic interest in the three-and-a-half years of court martial turned up high when the military acquitted Lou and Phil's killer, and even higher when I gave a copy of the covered-up guilty plea to The New York Times.

But in the years since, my media appearances came and went as we waged an on-again, off-again war to convince the military Lou deserves a Purple Heart.

The topic of the Purple Heart is long and complex, so I will just lay the highlights down here for context.

The military labeled Lou's death as nonhostile. It does not believe that a member of the United States military who willfully murdered two fellow soldiers—his own officers—is an enemy of our country. The military told us this again and again. It also failed to acknowledge the other argument: since technically it declared the killer not guilty, it could not then turn around and say Lou and Phil were not killed by a more politically correct and accepted version of the enemy to meet the requirements for a hostile death classification.

In the fifteen years since Lou and Phil were killed, over a dozen attempts have been made by me and Lou's sister and parents, to convince the army to change Lou's death certificate to Hostile, and award him the Purple Heart.

Why does this matter, you ask?

Lou's legacy matters to us. Acknowledging that a soldier who willfully kills other soldiers in a combat zone is an enemy of our country matters to us. If the 42nd Infantry Division had trained its soldiers to recognize the danger before them as real, Lou and Phil would still be alive. Similar threats were overlooked in similar cases. Those are the most important reasons. There are several subsets of importance stemming off those, and I readily talk about them in other forums, but we'll leave that part of this here for now.

On that particular spring day, I was in the midst of another campaign to right this wrong. This time I had more help.

Two Vietnam veterans, William "Monsoon" Mimiaga and Medal of Honor recipient John Baca, were driving cross-country getting signatures on a petition for me. I was simultaneously launching a White

House online petition in the hopes of gathering 100,000 signatures, which would force a discussion.

Some news outlets were willing to help, and that week one of the networks was sending a reporter and cameraman to my house. I knew I had a lot of work to do to make my house presentable. I'd cleared the entire day's schedule to get rid of pet fur, laundry, and the general mess that comes from a single mom raising four boys and a zoo on her own.

The reporter sounded like she had more to say than just confirming our interview, but I would have to get the dogs quieted down before I had a chance to hear her. Holding my phone in one hand and clutching my towel with the other, I ran downstairs toward the back door, and froze in total shock as my eyes locked with a strange man entering my kitchen through my sunroom door.

The entire world froze for a nanosecond.

The fear hit me first. I was naked under a small towel, sopping wet, and unarmed. I was alone in my home and a man I'd never seen before was about eight feet away from me, entering my kitchen. All my amazing guard dogs were outside uselessly barking, leaving me extremely vulnerable.

But the fight immediately rushed in, kicking fear right out of me and onto the intruder, whose horrified face spun around as he bolted out the door.

"Who the fuck are you?" I screamed at him as he fled. I didn't care that I was naked and alone and I didn't even consider simply locking the doors behind him and calling the police. I was in full fight mode and I would have jumped on that guy in my natural splendor if I had caught him.

I literally felt like I was going to kill him or die trying, because no way was I going to let anyone think it was okay to enter my home uninvited.

In a matter of a few strides, I chased the intruder across the patio, around the corner into my driveway, and … into the news crew van, where the stunned reporter sat in the shotgun seat, phone in her hand, while my dogs barked around her door.

The intruder had been the cameraman, who was apologizing as fast as he could for scaring me. The interview, it turned out, was not the next day. It was that day, right then.

There I was, almost naked, clutching a teeny towel around me, hair dripping wet, screaming in rage and threatening to kill the cameraman with my bare hands.

It was not a great first impression.

It's hard to come back from a moment like that. It was even harder to know which one of us felt more awkward—me for threatening the cameraman's life in an almost-naked rage, the cameraman for opening the door to my kitchen and running for his life, or the reporter who had to run the interview after witnessing her cameraman fleeing from a screaming, sopping wet, almost naked guest she had to position as a grieving, heroic widow.

Even better— after we all stumbled our way through the interview, and before the dust settled from their vehicle peeling away down the road, I had to call them back because the cameraman had been in such a rush to get out of there that he'd forgotten his expensive tripod.

Aside from the realization that I should lock my doors, that incident taught me something important.

I realized that I was no longer the puddle of apathy I'd been. I realized that there was more fight in me than I'd known. I realized that I was capable of defending myself in person and that meant I was capable of fighting in general. I realized I wanted to live again; I wasn't just going through the motions.

That incident awakened my inner warrior. I know that word is really overused but it's still appropriate here. It's what stuck with me strongly enough to know self-defense had to be a part of the event my fiancé and I ran.

We are Strong is one of the achievements I am most proud of, and I can't wait to do again even better. My fiancé Dave (I'll share more of him later) and I had been talking for some time about all the things I wished I'd known, the skills I wished I'd had, and the impact that insight and those skills would have had on my boys and me if I'd possessed them earlier. Every day I hopped online or many times when I spoke with a fellow widow friend, I heard a different version of my own story: we were vulnerable, we had good hearts, we were struggling, and we were easy prey.

Predators love widows, especially widows with military benefits. Widows with financial benefits, who have good hearts, and who never imagine a person would take advantage of all those things are especially prime prey.

I knew I was in good company in terms of widows who experienced the abuse of trust that manifested in physical, emotional, financial, and mental abuse as well. In addition to that, I saw widows overwhelmed with their pain and completely lost as to how to channel that pain, or how to build or rebuild a career.

As discussed in an earlier chapter, there are many events and resources designed to comfort military widows and their children, and those are amazing. But I'd yet to see an event that played into strength in a practical sense as well as an emotional one.

Dave and I began talking about hosting our open event with business leaders to teach about corporate and entrepreneurial paths, mindset mavericks who brought recreation into healing, survivors of trauma to share insight and actionable steps to healing, and a basic self-defense class for the physical and mental impact that training would have.

Then came the day I saw my friend Taya post that the Patriot Tour was coming to New York City, about eighty miles from us. The Patriot Tour is an inspiring live event headlined by Marcus Luttrell (the Lone Survivor) and packed with a lineup of incredible, patriotic speakers. David Goggins, Chad Fleming, and Taya Kyle would all be speaking at this event.

I knew right then that this was the moment to build our event around. Dave didn't even blink when I told him I wanted to build, fund, fill, and run this event all within the six weeks between that moment and the night of the Patriot Tour.

God must have supported this insanity, because within days we'd found angels to fund the event and a place to host it. We had speakers and instructors readily agree to participate for free. We had dozens of applicants from all over the country, and we had VIP passes to the Patriot Tour for all of them. David Lionheart was on board to bring his compassion and healing energy to the women just like he was doing in all of his Play For Your Freedom events he held for veterans and their families. Real estate investor Kent Clothier readily agreed to offer his extensive personal and professional resources to the women, and others in positions to offer their support did too.

This is where I need to give a major shout-out to the Got Your Back Network and the Committee for Families of War Veterans. I have long-standing relationships with those organizations. At one point I was a beneficiary of their support. Now I am on the boards of both and have the honor of being a small part of connecting others with that same support. Like Dave, neither blinked when I asked them for substantial donations to fund this event. These are some of the people who live with faith in their hearts, and whom God graciously placed in my path.

Just a few short months before our event, a military plane had crashed, killing seventeen service members. Some were still not old enough to legally buy a beer, but they'd lost their lives in service to our country.

Many of the fallen were local. Our attendees included the fiancée of one and the moms of others. Additionally, another young widow flying in from Utah was just months into her own loss. These women in particular were at risk for feeling indifferent to their own well-beings. Some of our other attendees entrusted us by sharing that they struggled with apathy and even suicidal thoughts because of the enormous pain they were in.

This is where the self-defense component of our event came in.

Eric Basek is a former SWAT officer—Top Shot, at that. He's also a CrossFit Level 3 trainer and an MMA instructor who holds two black belts in Krav Maga. He owns and runs Blue Titan Fitness in New Jersey. I interviewed Eric for American Snippets. We stayed in touch, and he instantly agreed to volunteer his expertise to come kick some widows to the mat for me.

It was absolutely incredible to see his session have exactly the impact I'd hoped it would: the women, when faced with a decision to allow themselves to be dropped to the mat, placed in a chokehold, or to defend themselves, defended themselves every time. They paid close attention to his instruction and followed it precisely. They threw themselves—literally—into this session.

Women who had just weeks before buried their sons or fiancés, women who were less than a year into their worlds as widows and single moms, women who had been trapped in inertia or convinced they no longer held any value for their own lives came face-to-face with those emotions on the mats. Every single one of them experienced a profound moment where they reconnected with their will to live.

We didn't have to break them down to build them up; they were already shattered in such painful ways when they arrived. But some part of them held the courage to come to that event. That alone was enough for me to believe there was a spark of will inside of them to survive, even if they didn't know it themselves.

When that courage was tested, it roared. I can still hear the grunts of fists hitting protective pads, as women who'd just met took turns punching the shit out of one another. I can hear the laughs as Eric yelled to us that we weren't trying to kick our attackers in the groin—we were kicking them in the faces, and their groins were just in the way. I can feel the energy in the room as one by one, the women left it all on the mat.

All the rage, all the hopelessness, all the helplessness, and all the doubt they had what it takes to turn the tables on their pain fell with their sweat and tears.

It was more than an introductory class in self-defense. It was an introduction to the new version of themselves as more than widows or grieving moms—they realized they had warrior hearts too.

They'd found their fight and they were ready to bring that fight to their grief.

The three-day event concluded with a trip to Manhattan to attend the Patriot Tour. We were able to bring them backstage to a photo-op with the speakers. Chad Fleming told the packed theater that there were Gold Star women in the audience, and thousands of hands clapped to honor the men we represented and in shows of support for all of us. It was beautiful and inspiring, and the feedback we got from the women was overwhelming.

That event taught me as much as it did our attendees. It taught me that when you are powered by faith, mountains can be moved. It taught me that crazy does not mean impossible. It taught me that teaching lessons I've learned can have a profound impact on the lives I reach. It taught me that warrior hearts are often disguised as broken hearts.

None of the women who attended that event returned home magically healed. None of them experienced magical transformations that produced instant and obvious rewards. In fact, some of them struggled with the weight of their breakthroughs, but the impact the event had on them helped them all shift their perspectives on life. It also forged some new friendships among them.

We made an effort to remain connected to all of our attendees. Six months after the event, we mailed them each the letter they'd written to themselves as one of their final exercises of the weekend. We connected with some of them online and saw some of them locally. But as time passed and all of our lives evolved and the world continued to spin, they moved forward on their paths, and we moved forward on ours, with only occasional communications with some of them.

Before that contact ebbed, though, we learned that they'd left our event with new awareness, new perspective, and new belief that they would find their paths across the challenges before them.

We saw some of them open businesses, or find new love, or create new traditions with their families—none of which any of them believed they would ever do when they came to us.

We don't for a second believe our event is what created those things for them. What we do know, though, is that the breakthroughs they each courageously experienced at our event ignited sparks in their spirits, which they then fanned into flames.

I credit the fight part of that event with being the most impactful moment. Without the opportunity to discover they had that fight within themselves, they would not have been able to open themselves up to absorbing the rest of the experience. From real estate investment to mindfulness to resilience to fitness and camaraderie, until they realized they wanted to make the most of the experience, they were attending it in a one-dimensional capacity. Tapping into the will to not just survive but to conquer is a game-changer.

105

The fight response does not just apply in literal life-or-death situations. Once you understand how to recognize the moments when your behavior is predicated on the fight-or-flight response, you are better able to make conscious decisions to stop allowing flight to keep you trapped in pain, inertia, or fear.

Think of something in your life that you have to tackle that you are either dreading or procrastinating.

Ask yourself these questions:

Why am I dreading this?
Why haven't I done this yet?
What will happen if I do not do this?
What will happen when I do?
How do I feel when I think of doing this?

When you think of this task or challenge, whether it is balancing your budget, breaking up with your significant other, asking for a raise, applying for a job, or cleaning your closet, do you get a knot in your stomach? Do you feel your pulse quicken, or your head throb, or your jaw clench, or any other physical response? Break it down and ask yourself what the worst possible outcome of getting that thing done is, and what the worst possible outcome of not doing it is. Which is worse?

Think of the worst thing that happened in your life. Did it sting? Did it hurt? Did it bring you to your knees?

Did you survive it? Are you here in this moment right now? If you had been asked before that last thing happened whether you could survive or overcome it, would you have said yes or no? If you are still in the middle of something catastrophic, the fact that you are here right now reading this book means that you have already survived longer than you thought you would after a nightmare becomes a reality. Let that wash over you for a minute. Let yourself tap into the extreme strength it took you to move past that moment.

That's your fight. That's the place you need to go every day to tap into whatever level of fight you need to meet that moment. Even on days you have no crisis—maybe even especially on the days you have no crisis—go to that place and tap into your fight. Take that with you out into your day. Aim it at either a challenge or a goal, and get it done.

Chapter 9
Angels Among Us

I believe there are angels among us
Sent down to us from somewhere up above
They come to you and me
> *In our darkest hours*
> *To show us how to live*
> *To teach us how to give*
> *To guide us with the light of love....*

Lyrics from the Alabama hit song, "*Angels Among Us*"

It would help, reading this chapter, if you took a moment to Google that song and really pay attention to it. Close your eyes, hear the lyrics, let them connect with you as you open your mind up to what comes next.

I'll wait while you do that ...

(Of course, you don't have to do this. It's only for the people who really enjoy going just a step further than most others.)

I've always loved that song, for no particular reason. It was released before I met Lou and well before I began noticing or even thinking about the angels in our lives.

Now, before you skip this chapter because you don't believe in angels, hear me out.

Whether you believe in God, Buddha, Allah, any other version of God, or no God at all—if you are truly open-minded and receptive to the concept that there are things about this world and this life that none of us truly understands, you will then be able to consider and accept the notion that you have experienced moments inspired by a power or energy outside of our normal consciousness.

Still with me?

Déjà vu, for instance. Who has not lived through a moment that they recognized, where they knew exactly what they would see, hear, smell, touch, taste, or say in that moment? Weird, isn't it?

Or maybe you explain that away through science rather than buy into the possibility that there is more to it.

How about other things, like a feeling that you should ease up on the gas pedal a split second before a deer you didn't see bolts in front of you? Or a total stranger coming up to you in a difficult moment and saying something that is so profound and powerful it moves you to tears? What about the stories of strangers happening upon an accident and jumping in to save the life of a person they don't know?

And so on.

Take a moment now to think about your own life. What moment did you have that you felt like you narrowly avoided an accident or sensed something was wrong just in time to prevent something terrible happening? Can you consider the possibility that there was some version of an angel whispering into your ear, or someone else's ear, that prompted them to act?

Angels don't have to be majestic, winged visions of beauty descending in beams of light for all to see. They make their presence known through energy instead of stage presence. They don't have to perform miracles or call attention to themselves. Instead, they prefer to work through us or, at least, through the people whose hearts are open to their energy. These people are the conduits for the work of angels. They can be everyday people like any one of us. I don't think they are even aware that they are channeling grace on such a high level. They simply lead with their hearts, which are being guided by the grace of angels. They can slip in and out of our lives in a moment or walk with us through life.

At least, that's what I believe.

Here are some of the people I swear have been led by angels straight into my life.

A few weeks before the uniformed men rang my doorbell, a handful of other strangers did. These men were Vietnam veterans. Somehow they'd heard that Lou was up at Fort Drum preparing to deploy. They'd heard that I was home with four small children and that a shady contractor had torn apart the only bathroom we had on the main floor of our home. They knew that contractor left a hazard zone in place of a bathroom before pocketing the money we'd scrounged up for the renovations and faded into the night.

"Ma'am," one of the men explained to me, "Lou is our brother." They asked me if I would allow them to repair the damage done and complete the job. For several days, the men came and went, quietly working together like an elite team.

Lou was as stunned and moved as I was when I called to tell him. The relief and joy in his voice were unmistakable, and I hope those men understood the gift they gave him.

I know a lot of people. Lou knew even more, and between us we had dozens of friends and family members who could have completed this job, but we never asked any of them for help. No one I knew owned up to sending those men to our home and all they would tell me is they "heard their brother was deploying and his family needed some help." They'd simply answered the call. That was all I ever got out of them.

Before long, the job was complete and the danger zone in front of my bedroom had been converted into a beautiful bathroom with a sunken, jetted tub. The veterans vanished as abruptly as they'd appeared, brushing off my thanks as they exited my home.

I never got the chance to enjoy that tub. Not once, because just a few days later my doorbell rang again, and this time it was the men in uniform telling me Lou was dead.

Still, those men—I believe they were led to me by angels—gave Lou a gift of peace. They gave me the inspiration to stop feeling so alone and misunderstood as I coped with Lou's deployment. After all, I told myself, these men suffered horrifically, first decades ago in a nightmarish war and again when they were villainized upon returning home. They had absolutely every right to leave this generation to fend for itself, but instead they did things like step forward to take care of another man's family, because he was their brother.

As my home flooded with family in the immediate aftermath of Lou's death, I was extremely aware of how much worse it would have been if my main floor were still a shamble of drywall, buckets, pipes, and wires like it had been just a week or two before.

I still have no idea who those men were. I wouldn't recognize them if I bumped into them, and yet I will never forget them. They were the first angels I recognized in my life, but nowhere near the last.

Anyone who knows me knows that I become emotional when I talk about our Vietnam veterans. This is not to say all of our men and women who honorably serve and sacrifice are not special, but I do confess that, for me, the Vietnam veterans are just extra.

I believe many of them are guided by the grace of angels because I can't think of any other way a person could walk through the fires they have and emerge as warriors and also as beacons of hope, help, and inspiration for so many others.

There is an organization called Snowball Express (SBE) that my boys and I have been blessed to be a part of for over a decade. The second time Christmas without Lou rolled around, some of the widows I'd connected with online began talking about an invitation they'd received to fly out to California and spend a few days in December together with other widows and their children, in honor of the fallen and as a way to have help tapping into the Christmas spirit.

It seemed insane and suspicious, but a few of us decided to attend together with plans to buy our own return flights if things were not okay.

One day I took a chance and answered a call from an unknown caller. It was Roy White, a pilot and one of the volunteers involved in the event. He coordinated with all the families and welcomed us all when we arrived. Although it was exhausting and not without its glitches, the time we spent in California was one packed with beauty, emotion, and one precious moment after another where we—the widowed moms or dads—could drop our defenses and absorb the magnitude of what went on around us.

People came out and lined the streets with signs of support: Your Dad is a Hero! We will never forget! God Bless You! … One sign after another, held by one smiling or sometimes tearful face after another, as the buses we rode in passed by and the supporters saw tiny hands waving back at them from the windows.

Each year this event grows. It moved to Texas and then to Florida when the Gary Sinise Foundation took it under its wing. From riding roller coasters at Six Flags to having the grounds of Oakley headquarters open only for our families to special games for the kids and resources for the parents to connect with and now to Disney, every year thousands of children of the fallen, along with their surviving parent or a guardian, receive the royal treatment.

Lifelong friendships and even young love have bloomed from these gatherings. Professional opportunities and a network of support that feels like family are other ripple effects, and do you know who several of the hundreds of volunteers are?

Vietnam veterans. Many of whom we have grown close to and consider family now. William "Monsoon" Mimiaga and John Baca are two of these veterans who have become family. "Monsoon" is a Vietnam and Gulf War veteran who then became California's Teacher of the Year. He's a special kind of crazy—the way a person has to be to leave such a massive impact on the world—and we love him. John is a Medal of Honor recipient whose Aw, shucks demeanor belies a mischievous nature that you can't help but love. Jim Preston and his wife Clancy have also stuck with us, refusing to allow distance or life dissolve their support. (Scott Meade, Larry Shatto, and John Fenech—I didn't forget you!)

I don't know how else to describe all of these people—the people who come stand by the side of the road for hours just to wave as we drive by; those who cheer and welcome us at the airport or hotel; those who spend an entire year in meetings and conference calls planning this event; the flight crews who donate their vacation time to man our flights; and to Gary Sinise, who uses his platform, fame, and resources to carry this event and our families into the next era—other than as acting on the whispers of angels.

Some of those angels are scattered through the event each year. I compare them to Wi-Fi boosters, set up strategically around a home to make sure the signal bounces from one place to the next.

There are the weathered faces who have seen dark times and light up with warmth as they calm an overwhelmed mom. There are the flight attendants who know just what to say to a child who is nervous about flying, and there are the special guests who fly on random flights (most of these flights are now chartered through American Airlines and are entirely full of SBE families) and throw their own resources and talent behind it.

I could write an entire book on Snowball Express, from its inception to the stories of attendees and volunteers. There are lessons on magnanimity, humility, and resilience from attendees and volunteers right on up to donors or sponsors. They are important lessons that I am blessed to have received.

***

Another kind of angel is, I believe, the most frequent and the most frequently overlooked kind. These are the angels who slip in and out of our lives in a moment but whose message and light remain for a lifetime.

On June 15, 2005, as I sat in the car alongside my Casualty Assistance Officer, I was drowning in pain. We were on our way to the funeral mass for Lou, and if I could have crawled out of my own skin to join him in eternity I would have. I don't know how many cars were in that caravan of death, but the police cars and the Patriot Guard Riders all around us made sure we moved as one.

Traffic on the other side of the two-lane road crept along, one car after another with faces turned toward us—Lou's death was big news and everyone knew that this procession was for him.

It felt like we were moving tortuously slow and at lightning speed at the same time. Faces of people lining the streets with flags passed in a blur. Every minute closer to the church we got, my panic and pain increased. I did not want to do this. Help! If I jump out of this car at this speed, would it be enough to kill me or would it just ding me up a bit? Should I try anyway? No, I can't. My kids are in the car behind me, and they would literally run me over. I can't do that to them. Help me God. I am not strong enough for this. All of those things flew through my heart and my mind, screaming in my head as I stared out the window until I almost broke down in tears.

And then I saw him.

WHAT NOT TO WEAR TO A MURDER TRIAL

I saw the John Deere green of his tractor first. It was a stark contrast from everything around us, just on the outskirts of a heavily built-up area. Minivans, cars, and pickup trucks snaked slowly through the congestion, tucked up tightly against one another. Their drivers were either curious as to the delay and the scene before them, or annoyed, or humbled. From my view behind tinted windows and tear-filled eyes, it was impossible to tell which—except for him.

The vividness of the colors struck me first, as my eyes traveled from the pavement to that recognizable green of his tractor to his blue denim jeans, to the rich darkness of his black skin straight on up to his yellow straw hat, all of which had a backdrop of a sky so blue and bright it stung my eyes even through the tint. The world slowed down even more until it seemed like a projectionist was creating a dramatic effect in real life. All noise around me disappeared, as my eyes reached his and seemed to meet his gaze. In a move that was strong and immediate while also appearing to be slow and subtle, he dropped his head and lowered his gaze to the ground in the faintest nod before his chin and eyes raised back up to look down from his tractor straight through that tinted window and into my eyes to speak to my soul.

I swear to you that in the course of those eight or maybe ten seconds, that man sent me an energy and a warmth that felt like it came straight from heaven. It was an unspoken message. It was the kind of message meant to be felt and experienced with my heart rather than heard with my ears, and I got that message louder and clearer than if it had been screamed through a bullhorn right in my face:

God is here with you. Grace is here with you, in this car, in this moment. It is all around you every minute of every day, but you have to be open to it to feel it.

It sounds crazy. I'm aware of that but I don't care because it's true. I told you in the beginning of this book that you have to decide to be open to accepting its message if you want to get the most out of it. This is your opportunity to do so, or your excuse to laugh and walk away. I can lead you to thought but I can't make you think. It may even sound hypocritical or shocking to those who know me and know I haven't set foot in a church in over a decade. But those who know me well, know that when I extracted religion from my faith, my faith blossomed.

To each their own, right?

Whether I die today or live another fifty years (that's a pretty optimistic number, given I'm not too far from fifty right now!), I will never forget that man, that angel who came to me exactly when I needed him. My presence at the funeral and the days after may not have displayed the grace that was imparted to me, but that grace is what kept me on my feet and allowed me to stumble through it all.

The next quick visit I got from an angel came fairly quickly. It was just about six or seven weeks after that funeral procession. I was at the shore with my kids and my family on the trip we'd planned for months and which I figured would be good for my kids to still experience. So as much as it hurt pretty much every minute of every day, I did manage to appreciate any time one of my kids laughed.

But I still wished I would die.

It was on the way home from that trip that the next angels appeared.

I was not looking forward to the four-hour drive home. That wasn't unusual for me, because I didn't look forward to anything anymore, other than seeing my husband's killer die. While I watched all my sisters pack up with their husbands and their kids, and my parents pack up and drive away together, I was feeling mighty depressed and mighty sorry for myself that I was all alone again. I mean, I had always known I would physically be on this trip alone with my boys because Lou would be in Iraq. But emotionally, I would have been able to call my husband and the kids would have been able to talk with their dad and our family would have still been intact. I was used to that and it was still hard, but it had nothing on the kind of hard this was.

Loneliness attacked me. I just let it in as I drove. My own little angels were all content for the moment. They were the good kind of tired. They were chatty and giggly and sleepy as they settled in for the drive, completely unaware that their mother was waging a war between her love for them and her complete disconnection from any other joy in life.

Boom!

The front right tire blew out right in the midst of concrete barrier construction traffic.

Fucking fantastic.

The feel of the van made it abundantly clear that I was riding on the rim. There would be no grace distance to find a safe pullover spot.

I was faced with taking my four boys out of the van and perching them on top of the concrete barrier while I attempted to squeeze between the tire and concrete and hope that no one clipped the side of the van as they passed, or leave them in the van as I handled things and prayed.

In that moment, it never occurred to me to have all of us stay in the van, turn on the hazards and call for backup to help make this a safe tire change in the middle of all that traffic.

Hazards on, emergency brake on, kids movie on, I told the boys to sit tight while mommy fixed the tire and chatted with them as I tossed all our crap off the top of the spare tire compartment and threw it all under the van.

I wasn't sure exactly how to change this particular tire, so I called my parents, who were not that far ahead of me, and they began the drive back to help out. In the meantime, I started setting things up.

"Excuse me ma'am, can I help?"

I nearly jumped right out into the slow-moving traffic and splatted on the hood of an annoyed passerby's car when I jumped from the sound of the voice. I hadn't even heard his car stop or him come up behind me.

There he stood, in a light business suit, gleaming shoes, and perfect hair, in front of his luxury car. I couldn't believe he would be willing to get those clothes and hands dirty, or risk the perils of traffic, to help me.

He insisted, gently, saying if it was his mom or sister with her kids, he'd want someone to do the same. He told me it was a two-man job—someone had to wave traffic around the van so no one got killed.

I smiled an inward, ironic grin at that one, and took my post guarding this man's life. My parents pulled up just as he drove off. Somehow, he'd preserved his pristineness in the task and had departed as immaculate looking as he'd arrived.

Another angel I had almost forgotten about.

My parents said hello and goodbye to the boys and me. My dad reminded me that the donut tire was not intended for long distances or high speeds, and I promised to be extra careful. They drove off and I pulled out behind them, focusing on silencing my soft sobs of overwhelmed grief, loneliness, anger, sharpened awareness of vulnerability, and a whole bunch of other emotions. I didn't want my boys to feel like their mom couldn't handle whatever came our way. But I did need a break to regroup myself, so I pulled into the next rest stop and told them they could order whatever they wanted for lunch.

"Yay!" Another unexpected adventure for them. They laughed and jumped around as they emerged from the van. I carried Jeremy—he was just under two years old and apt to tear off like a dog chasing a squirrel. Great, I thought. How the fuck am I supposed to manage all four of these guys? Trevor was six. Colin was five. Sean had just turned four, and our youngest, who still has the nickname Menace, was not quite two. This presented quite a challenge in a packed rest stop. Again, the despair and enormity of my life hit me.

My boys seemed to instinctively pick up on the fact that in situations like this, I needed them to be on their absolute best behavior. Getting them to the bathroom, and then to the food counter, and then seated at a table together seemed to go much more smoothly than I'd anticipated but still, as I sat there with the four of them, all I saw was the empty seat at the table and all I felt was the gaping wound in my heart.

That's when she happened by.

I saw her as she approached. I noticed her soft smile before I noticed her gently weathered face, the silvery white of the loose hair that refused to remain in a bun, and the ever-so-slight hunch in her aged shoulders. She walked alone, holding her tray and food. She walked with intent through the people around us, straight up to our round table.

Her smile reached right through the darkness I was wrapped in and her quiet voice somehow pierced the noise of the crowd.

"You have a beautiful family," she said as she leaned over my son's shoulder to look me directly in the eye.

Her smile seemed ageless. The warmth and energy she sent me washed right through my invisible wall of pain and grief that she'd somehow been able to see when no one else had.

Before I stuttered out a thank you, she was gone. She moved quickly. In a moment, she was swallowed up in the crowd and I almost thought I'd imagined her. But I knew she'd been real.

The boys were unaware of the interaction or the tears I couldn't stop from slipping out of my eyes.

It was another profoundly powerful experience for me. It made me sit up, breathe deeply, and look around the table at the four little lives I was entrusted with as if I hadn't really been able to see them before.

"I do have a beautiful family," I whispered, as the awareness of that fact crashed into me.

The rest of our drive home was smooth and quiet. My anger and fear no longer rode shotgun with me. Instead, I felt like there was a new presence sitting quietly beside me, kind of like my German Shepherd does when he wants to let me and any stranger who approaches me know that I am not alone and backup is available if I need it.

I've had other angels appear over the years. Sometimes they work through ordinary people, as in the instances I just shared. Other times they appear as thoughts, or instincts, or small miracles. I cannot count the number of times I've been driving when I felt the need to look to the side for a moment, just as another car ran through a light or a stop sign. Or even when I feel like I should slow down for a second, and a deer runs right in front of me instead of me slamming into it. I have actually looked into an empty shotgun seat and high-fived an imaginary guardian angel beside me. I've looked to the sky and recommended that whoever my guardian angel was that day gets a bigger halo.

Yes, I realize this will all sound crazy to some people but, before you dismiss it as such, answer this for me: would you rather walk through life with a heart and mind open to the potential of angels you would otherwise miss, or walk through it with a closed heart and mind, and risk missing them?

I invite the believers and challenge the doubters to do the same exercise right now. Make everything around you in this moment disappear in your mind so you are focused only on this. Close your eyes if you need to. Take some deep breaths, or whatever gets you to be laser-focused on this task.

Think very thoroughly through the last five years of your life. Flip through your memories until you land on a moment when something a stranger said or did made you feel differently than you had a moment ago. Maybe you are someone this is easy for—maybe a stranger literally happened upon you in a life-or-death moment and saved you. That's awesome, but that's also too easy. Think harder, past that moment, for a more subtle angel.

Or maybe you are the opposite. Maybe no one has ever been there for you. Maybe you have been alone and victimized and feel abandoned by everyone and everything. That's also too easy to use as an excuse to dismiss this concept. You, too, need to think harder for a few minutes.

Whatever angle you approach this from, the exercise is the same: open your mind and your heart. Break down seemingly ordinary moments in any kind of day, good or bad. Most often these will be bad moments or will hold the potential to become bad moments. Were you driving your car when someone just missed slamming into you? Were you stressed or sad when a stranger smiled at you or offered you a compliment? Were you broke and scared when someone stepped up to offer you support? Did you ever have a gut feeling that compelled you to do something that wound up being a huge moment for you? Were you ever in the midst of an agonizing moment when you noticed something beautiful?

If you truly dig deep into your memories with an open heart and mind, you will recognize a moment when your actions or the actions of others came from a place you did not create. Rather, they came from a place you were open to receiving.

If you're with me this far, you can go one step further and ponder this: perhaps there was a moment in someone else's life, when that angel was you.

Chapter 10
I Believe

This seems like the perfect time to roll into this next topic. If you're still with me after the chapter on angels, that must mean at least a small part of you is open to believing in something bigger than all of us.

That's good because we are taking it up a notch here.

Let's talk about death and what comes after that.

If I close my eyes and take myself back a lot of years, I can still see my maternal grandmother's excited smile. At first, I was surprised to see her perched at the end of my bed. I'd fallen into an exhausted sleep after another full day of a packed college course load and two of my four part-time jobs.

She'd been asleep when I stopped in to see her on my way to bed. She'd stirred and tried to sit up when I called her name. She also tried to speak but could not, and I'd jumped back in horror when she opened her eyes and I saw how yellow they'd turned. So how could she be here in my room now?

"Barbara," she said in the way she did when she was full of energy, more like a song than regular speech. Her white summer nightgown hung loosely and the light around her seemed to shine from within instead of upon her. That was weird, I thought. In fact, all of this was weird. How had she managed to get up here at all? She'd finally dropped into the appearance of a peaceful coma after the final tormented days of her several-years-long struggle against a rare cancer. How could she have gotten up, dressed in a new nightgown, done her hair, returned color to her face, and chased the jaundice yellow from her crystal-clear blue eyes?

What was happening here—was I dreaming?

My bed creaked a bit as she leaned in toward me with a laugh on her lips. "I have to go now, honey. I knew you'd wake up if I came and told you. Tell everyone I said goodbye." The sheer joy coming from her was incredible.

Now I was completely bewildered. I rubbed my eyes to wake myself up, and she was gone. My head had just returned to my pillow when the hall light beamed into my eyes, waking me back up.

"Barbara," my mom's voice called to me. Contrary to my grandma's voice, my mom sounded broken and exhausted. My confusion was absolute.

"Grandma is gone," she said, as she encouraged me to come say goodbye.

I automatically got up without saying a word. I don't know if my mom noticed my lack of surprise or not. I was thinking, I know she left. She just told me she was leaving! But as I walked through my door and into the hallway, I stepped back into real life and remembered that in this real life, we'd been watching the grandma we loved slowly lose all joy and all ability to manage her pain. For years we'd nursed her and cared for her and cried for her as we watched cancer's merciless campaign on her body. Until recently, her spirit had withstood that onslaught where her body could no longer, but the last words I heard her say from her bed were words begging God to let her die.

More to make my mom feel better than for me, I obediently went downstairs to the living room and stood beside my grandmother's ravaged body. There was no energy in that room. Only emptiness. I said, "Goodbye, Gram," or something like that and went back upstairs.

I was awake the rest of the night trying to figure out what I had experienced. By the time morning came, I convinced myself I had just dreamed it all, and I never mentioned it to anyone. To this day, I have shared it with only a handful of people.

Given the intensity of that moment and the ones to follow, I am now convinced it was real.

My next experience in this realm came when I watched my grandpa die. This was my dad's dad. He was ninety-six years old, I believe, and quite the character. I imagine he was tough to be raised by, but to me and my siblings he was a good mix of a stern and loving grandfather. He'd served as a chief deputy inspector in the NYPD until he got swept up in the arbitrary fallout of the Knapp Commission. As long as I remembered him, he'd been retired, and divided his time between his Queens brownstone and his little trailer in Florida.

He'd maintained his independence and his mind admirably for years since his wife, my other grandma, died, but for the last few years of his life he'd lived with us. Slowly he lost pieces of himself until he became dependent on us. I was married then, with four small children, one of whom was not yet a year old. I'd just recovered from a severe case of pancreatitis, which included emergency surgeries, early liver failure, and months of treatment. My husband was in the National Guard and often away when he was not at his high school teaching job. I would fill in as needed, especially if my parents stepped away for a rare day or two to themselves. I would bring grandpa his lunch, help him change his soiled clothes if he'd had an accident, and wash up.

Part of me realized he was physically declining, but I was still caught off guard when the call came that he was in the hospital.

I don't remember how many days he was in the hospital, only that he was not conscious for any of them, as far as I recall. Definitely not when I visited him.

It was brutal for my father. He was the one left to decide on the measures to take, to prolong Grandpa's life or not. My six siblings and I came and went over the days, but my dad was there the most with my mom.

Finally the day arrived when the doctors said my grandfather was actively dying. His breathing had changed into the Cheyne-Stokes pattern that signaled death's imminent arrival.

I remember standing on the edge of the crowded room, close to the door, and observing the scene. Almost everyone was crying or wiping quiet tears. I was not.

I almost felt like I was crazy again because instead of sadness, I felt joy. I felt a warmth and a light and I imagined my grandfather's own mother was in that room smiling at her son and telling him it would be okay.

Even as I write this, I feel a little crazy and maybe even a little uncertain about sharing it because the insecure side of me is screaming at me to hit delete immediately.

But as sure as you are reading these words, I felt that joy just like I had when my grandmother sat on my bed to say goodbye. Two completely different experiences with the same unexpected arrival and the same level of unfiltered joy.

It felt so strong and in such stark comparison to what I knew I was supposed to be feeling that I started to feel like an asshole. What was wrong with me? Why wasn't I sad? I loved my grandpa and it also sucked to see my normally serious and unemotional dad break down crying.

I thought if I took a walk and came back, the feeling would be gone and I'd be able to feel properly sad, but nope. It was still there when I returned. So I just gave in to it, quietly.

I imagined a conversation with the great-grandma I'd never met and I let myself believe that she was indeed there. I let myself believe that while my grandpa's body lie still on that bed, his spirit was beginning to dance.

It was literally one of the most beautiful moments of my life. I don't know why I felt it, or why no one else did. Maybe I am just crazy.

But wait … there's more.

June 7, 2005 started on a happy note. I managed to video chat with Lou, who was in Iraq. I brought the four boys in with me to see their dad on the computer screen and say hello.

One by one they squirmed around in front of the camera so their dad could see them too. Our youngest, Jeremy, was three months shy of his second birthday. He was just beginning to put words together, but he absolutely knew who that man on the computer screen was.

"Mommy!" he exclaimed as he spun in my arms to make sure he had my attention. "Daddy!" He squealed and laughed the word out while pointing from me to the computer screen. Yes, buddy. Lou and I laughed together—it's Daddy!

This memory is a painful one for me to relive and to write, but it comes into play in a way that even the biggest skeptic reading this will have a difficult time explaining away.

The chat flew by. I only had a few minutes before I had to get our oldest son Trevor on the bus for his day at kindergarten.

"I love you," we said to each other as we smiled our goodbyes and ended the chat. I was already looking forward to our scheduled call again that night. I missed that man deeply.

That day I decided to do something I had not done in years—literally—and definitely not when I was on my own while Lou was actively deployed. I decided to take the morning to step away from my responsibilities.

I knew Lou was going to call me that night (his time in Iraq, but late afternoon in New York), and I couldn't wait to catch up on things. I had time, I thought, before the call. So I stopped at my sister's house to have lunch with her and our mom.

Midway through lunch, as we sat in the warm June sun and I actually started to relax, my phone rang. Caller ID showed the random numbers that meant it was from Iraq. It was Lou! I jumped up to answer but service was terrible there, and the call dropped before either of us could speak.

I was instantly frantic.

After about an hour of trying to pretend I was not upset, I began the hour drive home. Our amazing babysitter had the kids and I knew they were fine, but still I felt an urgency to get home in case Lou called again.

Here's where it happened.

Sometime around 2:30, I was driving down the street in Milford, Pennsylvania. Our home was about fifteen minutes away. As I glanced out the passenger window, I could have sworn I saw Lou's face sort of superimposed over someone else's as a man walked down the sidewalk. Before I could process that weird sight, I felt Lou sitting next to me in the shotgun seat. As I looked over, I saw him in my mind. His face was drained of all color. In my mind I heard him say, "Oh shit!" as fear flicked through his normally smiling hazel eyes. And then he was gone. Or it was gone. My car was empty except for me. There was no one riding shotgun and no hint of Lou or anyone who looked like him walking down the sidewalk.

But now I was operating on terror. I felt something was terribly wrong.

The roads back to that house are windy and can be slow when caught behind someone. I pushed it as fast as I could and ran into our house. Our babysitter told me Lou had just called. I'd missed him again. He'd called about an hour ago, she said. Which meant about forty-five minutes before I'd felt whatever I'd felt while driving.

I'm just crazy, I told myself. I'm sure he's fine. But I carried our phone around with me every minute for the rest of the day and night.

Just when I began to get a lid on my inner hysteria, I was hit from nowhere with another nauseating punch. All four kids were seated at our kitchen table. I was handing one of them a bowl of mac and cheese when it physically felt like I'd been punched right in my gut.

I actually fell forward onto the table and dropped the dish. My kids looked at me with concern. "Are you okay, mommy?"

I was not okay, but I had no idea why. According to our microwave clock, it was 5:22 p.m.. Iraq is seven hours ahead of us, so why hadn't Lou called again? I had the computer volume cranked in our first-floor bedroom and I checked it every five minutes to be sure I didn't miss the beep that signaled his call.

The rest of that night crept by. I only half-slept until my doorbell rang at 6:00 a.m., and the military detail told me Lou had been killed in Iraq.

As the weeks and months unfolded, we received a timeline of events. When I'd been driving through town and felt Lou in the car with me, it had been right around the time of the explosion, in which Lou was mortally wounded. He'd been conscious for a couple hours, in pain, and aware that he was dying.

When I'd been serving my kids mac and cheese, Lou's chest had been cracked open and his heart beat for the last time in the hands of a doctor.

I am sharing these experiences not so much to tell you what I believe they mean, but to invite you to decide that for yourself. Here is another one.

Later in the day on June 9, as family gathered and the CAO arrived, Jeremy ran across the yard to me. As usual, he had nothing but a diaper and a smile on and I swept him up as he yelled, "Mommy!" Then, he wiggled around in my arms to look me right in the eye and point at me as he said, "Mommy!" again. Immediately after he yelled my name, he pointed toward the sky in exactly the same way he'd pointed at the computer screen while Lou was on it. "Daddy!" he yelled.

He repeated this three or four times, pointing to me as he yelled, "Mommy!" and to the sky as he yelled, "Daddy!"

He was still too young to have any clue what had happened. He had no way to know that his daddy was gone—forever—and he had no inkling what the word heaven was. But there you have it. Just like I know I saw and felt those things I did on June 7, I know my son saw his daddy in the sky that day.

That's what I believe, anyway. What about you?

I wasn't seeking those experiences. Quite the opposite. Each time they occurred, I was completely focused on the moment I was in— sleeping, or driving, or enjoying lunch, or wallowing in my own pain. There were other experiences over the years with my kids. There was the time Jeremy (still under two years old) cracked up loudly in his sleep so hard that he had to catch his breath before yelling, "Daddy!" It was as if he was being tickled, as he rolled around laughing and calling his dad's name. There was the time I was driving when, out of the blue, my son Sean, then four years old, suddenly yelled out, "Mommy! Daddy's here! Can you see him? He's holding your hand, Mommy!"

Over the years the boys had those moments, less and less with time. They all happened with no context to their dad; they were completely spontaneous.

One experience for me was the exception to that. It was the night of June 9, 2005, the day after the military arrived at my door. I was outside on our glider swing, wrapped in a blanket, rocking and crying. I was talking to God, talking to Lou at the same time, trying to make sense of any of it. But the only thing I felt was excruciating pain from the depths of my core, the kind there is no relief from. The kind that makes you beg to die if that is the only way out from under it.

Suddenly, the pain ceased. In its place came a rush of warmth and peace so brilliant and so strong it took my breath away, too, but in a good way. It brought tears to my eyes with its intensity and all I could think was that I would give anything for it to never end.

It lasted maybe two or three minutes, until the front door opened and my sister-in-law came out to check on me. The feeling swooshed right out of me like an exhale, but when I inhaled again the pain was not there either. Instead, there was a merciful numbness that I readily sank down into until the headlights of our newspaper delivery guy pierced the serenity, and I saw the boys and me on the front page.

I don't know how I would respond to someone sharing these experiences with me if I had not experienced them myself. I've read the articles from scientists and experts explaining them away as creations of the subconscious. It's not for me to tell you what to believe or what to deduce from my experiences. I am sharing them because they led to me believing in the existence of life, or energy, after death. They gave me a comfort and a certainty that have never left, no matter how much time passes or what difficulties I have faced. If they can do that for me, maybe they can for you too. Or maybe you have also had similar experiences and you also tell yourself you are crazy.

I don't pretend to have supernatural powers or to be a spiritual guru or to have some sort of ability to have actual conversations with dead people, or any of that. What I am saying, though, is that I am 100% certain there is an energy and a level of life beyond what we see physically in front of us. It is present to those who are open to feeling it, even if we are not actively seeking it. It appears in the purest of moments, to the purest of minds in that moment—minds that are unobstructed by anything other than energy and profoundness.

These experiences have instilled a spirituality in me that a childhood of church and Catholic school did not. On the contrary, they repaired damage to my spirituality that was inflicted through those experiences. It is that spirituality I tap into on a regular basis, when I am grateful for a moment or an event, or when I am hurting or afraid or angry or stressed. I always reach back from physical emotions for that spiritual perspective, and it has served me well.

I invite you to do the following:

Have open, honest conversations with a friend or family member on this topic. Maybe in a group setting or maybe one-on-one. Maybe go nuts and pose the question on social media: "Who has had an experience related to feeling an energy around a death?" or something of that nature and see what you get back. And if you have had such an experience, be brave. Lead the way with that statement and share that experience before asking the question. My bet is you won't even have to ask the question at all because someone, or more than one person, will pipe up with their story all by themselves.

You can accept that invitation or decline it. I can't make that choice for you. But if you are leaning toward declining it, ask yourself this first: Are you completely convinced it is not possible, or are you just worried about what people will think of you?

Chapter 11
Words of Wisdom

No doubt, people said a lot of stupid shit to me after Lou died. They all meant well. Maybe for some people the comments would indeed have been comforting or inspiring.

"You're young and pretty—you'll find someone else one day."

"At least you're used to being alone because Lou was gone so much already."

"I know how you feel. My (aunt, grandma, dog, etc.) died last year."

"He's in a better place."

"It's time for you to get over it."

"I know how hard it is to be a single mom. I feel like a single mom because my husband works so much."

"It must be nice to have that insurance money."

For me, I pretty much wanted to bitch-slap every person who said these things to me.

I'm just keeping it real here. I never pretended to be flawless.

But in the midst of the well-intended or just casual statements, some people offered me words of advice or issued challenges that wound right through the clusterfucks in my mind to hit me right in the heart. They were game changers for me. Maybe something in here will be for you too.

It is natural to hold on to guilt. I can't tell you how many combat veterans I have met whose guilt is a tangible presence. When I speak at events for veterans, I always make it a point to tell them that no matter what happened, no matter what situation led to the combat deaths they continue to feel responsible for, they are not at fault. I pull out the words Elaine, the grief counselor I mentioned earlier, said to me. I use them to help the veterans and ask them if they intended to see harm befall their brother or sister and remind them that they are not all powerful. They can lay down their pack now. I tell them that if the buddies they mourn were anything like Lou, the thing they would want most is to know the people they gave their lives alongside and in service of are making that sacrifice matter. If we choose to waste our lives wallowing in guilt, self-pity, bitterness, or anger, we are not truly honoring those sacrifices. Instead, we are deepening the pain and doing exactly what those who seek to destroy our country want to see happen—we are dragging ourselves and others around us down.

Those are harsh words, but I have never received anything but emotional hugs and thank yous after speaking them.

So I say to you too—whatever guilt you are carrying, real or imagined ways you let someone you love down—let it go. If you lost someone you love and carry guilt like I did, let it go. It does not serve you or their legacy to carry it. If you did actually wreak havoc and pain into the lives of others, you cannot alter that past, but you can learn and grow from it. You can seek forgiveness and strive to make up for it. Maybe forgiveness and the opportunity to repair the relationship will be granted. Maybe not. But the fact remains that you have the power to choose how you live each day forward. The best way you can make amends for that past, the best way to reclaim the potential in your own life, is to take a long, hard look at yourself and commit to making each day matter, from this minute on.

It is not an easy walk. I highly recommend anyone struggling with massive guilt or hopelessness and regret to find help learning how to let those go. Elaine was pivotal in my ability to do so but it was not a one-and-done cure for me. Over the years, I have surrounded myself with people who help me avoid falling back into those traps. Some are my friends. Others are people I follow and learn from virtually. Some are colleagues.

Some advice I blindly followed was horrible, like when the popular girl in high school pretended to befriend me just long enough to convince me that I should dump the only guy who ever asked me out. I spent the next three years repeatedly making an ass of myself trying to undo that. Be on the lookout for people like her—people who have a need to see you fail. They are in your life. I guarantee that.

Bad advice aside, I am forever grateful for the people who have given me amazing advice—even when it was hard to hear.

Terri Seifert is the widow of Army Captain Christopher Seifert. On March 23, 2003, Sgt. Hasan Akbar threw grenades into a tent of sleeping men on their base in Kuwait. He shot the soldiers as they fled the tent. Terri's husband was one of two men killed by Akbar, who also wounded fourteen others. Lou and I were stunned at the news reports of this attack. We followed the trial closely. Lou was impatient with the process and couldn't understand why Akbar was not shot on sight. Two months before Lou was killed, Akbar was found guilty and sentenced to death. That, said Lou, was the only appropriate outcome.

The case was fresh in my mind two months later. The attack had taken place on our wedding anniversary. I'd followed it with my husband and talked about it being the ultimate, worst betrayal of the oath to serve. The trial had taken place in Fort Bragg, and the prosecutor, Captain John Benson, was assigned to our case as well.

My mind and my heart were besieged with uncertainty, confusion, and fear. I didn't know a thing about military procedures outside of the death notification. I didn't know a thing about a murder trial, or being a widow, or any of it.

I needed some information and some support from someone who actually knew what I was facing. Someone who legitimately understood the shit show my world was and the arena I was about to enter. I couldn't count on the military; they'd already lied to me. I couldn't expect all the grieving people around me to have that information.

Terri Seifert was the only one who could be that resource.

My CAO honored my request to reach out to her. The day my phone rang and I heard her voice was the first time I felt understood. She knew what the courthouse looked like and what the courtroom was set up like. She knew the prosecutor was a good man. She knew how the media worked and what its interest was, and she knew what to expect in terms of lengthy processes and unanticipated delays.

131

Terri had a lot of powerful advice for me that day. But there was one thing in particular that made an immediate impact on me.

I told her that every time I managed to drift off to sleep, I would see Lou in the casket again. My mind would take me back to the funeral home. I would smell the sickeningly sweet lilies and feel the smooth wood of the casket under my hand. My knees would seem to shake as I saw the ball of dried glue that had been applied to keep Lou's eye closed. I would be right back there in that moment until I woke up in tears, hyperventilating. The alternate nightmare would be an explosion, and Lou bleeding against the wall, or talking about the boys and me as he was dying. Then I would spend the rest of the night emailing people or pacing the driveway under the stars with my dog Cassie watching over me.

I didn't know how to make that memory stop. I didn't know how to turn that endless loop off in my brain.

I don't remember Terri's answer verbatim, but I remember her point. She, too, had nightmares about her husband's murder. She had some advice for me, that another widow had offered her: they (our husbands) only experienced those moments once, and they would not want us to experience those moments at all, let alone repeatedly, even if just in our minds.

Would Lou want me to spend one second experiencing anything like he had?

The answer, of course, was no.

A weight lifted from me.

I kept Terri on the phone for a long time. She let me ask painful questions about her husband's murder and she opened up about very personal things she was experiencing. This was a woman whose own wounds were still very fresh. Her own world was still very raw and overwhelming. Yet she extended herself to me without a moment's hesitation. She remained available to me throughout the entire tortuous process of our court martial, the acquittal, and beyond. Gradually the roles blended, as we supported each other through issues outside of the trial. Over the years we've faded into our own lives, but either one of us can pick up the phone to call the other at any time, and we will answer.

Is there something in your life that you've allowed to plant a flag in your land, something that is always there and torments you? Did you experience a traumatic event, or a series of traumatic events, that remain present in your dreams or your conscious thought? Are your relationships with your sanity and well-being threatened by the force of those memories? Do they impact your behavior?

Wasn't experiencing it once enough? Isn't the time lost to it enough? Ask yourself, why are you putting yourself through the upset of reliving those moments?

PTSD is real. So are the symptoms. In the next chapter I'll talk about Post Traumatic Growth, but for now it's a good start to begin shifting that mindset that those nightmares or recurring thoughts and memories will always be a part of your life. Start telling yourself a new truth—that you will not let past experiences steal one more moment of peace from you. Start nourishing thoughts that involve you as the victor, instead of as the victim, of your own memories.

Energy goes where attention flows.

My work with American Snippets has opened up avenues for me to meet and build relationships with extraordinary people who exemplify resilience and courage. I am grateful for all of them, and I will share a list of some of the most powerful quotes from their interviews in a minute.

First, I am going to share some other words. These came from Lynda Roemer.

Lynda has been one of my best friends for, like, a really long time. Like I need four hands to count the years. Actually, I need five hands. More than one decade. You get the idea.

I met Lynda right after I married Lou—back when I didn't understand why facelifts are called facelifts, I could jump on a trampoline or cough without peeing, and I still believed evil only happened to other people.

Lynda and I have seen each other through marriage, divorce, death, abuse, injuries, parenting, step-parenting, triumphs, disasters, dating, and now a pandemic. Those are the highlights, anyway. She's the kind of friend who always gives you the truth, even if you don't ask for it.

Lynda was excited for me when I first met Mason. (That's not his real name, but it rhymes with his real name.)

Mason was good-looking, witty, fun, and great with my kids. He had the victim-to-victor story that made me believe in him as a person, and he made me laugh every day.

If I met him today, there would be a million sirens going off in my head. I am not the same naïve, trusting, gullible person I was back then. It never occurred to me that his entire story was pure fiction. I never imagined that his pretty face masked an ugly heart, and I never saw the disaster that was coming my way.

Neither did Lynda at first. But when the smiles faded and then turned into tears, Lynda noticed. When I told her the same excuses about Mason that she'd once used for her ex-husband, Lynda smelled bullshit. Other people did too, but they never pressed me on it. They never reminded me that I deserved better or, at least, I didn't deserve what he was doing to me and to my kids. Maybe they were afraid I'd blow up at them, or maybe they just didn't feel like dealing with it.

For a few years, Lynda was there to catch me when he knocked me down. Pretty much everyone but me, at that point, realized it was long past time to get him out of my life. But I felt responsible for him. I felt like it would break my kids' hearts to lose someone else.

Mason knew that about me. He worked it well. So did his mom, who told me if I left him, Mason would kill himself and it would be my fault.

Lynda was the only one I told the whole stories to. She knew he stole my money. She knew he was rough with me. She knew he passed out drunk and stole drugs from hospice patients. Some people knew some things. Lynda knew everything.

I had no idea how hard it was for her to watch this. I didn't know it was hurting her to pick me up from a parking lot where I was hiding from him and drop me off back home where she knew he'd be. I didn't realize she was emotionally exhausted from carrying my pain for years, until she said something to me that hit me like a jackhammer to my heart:

"Barb, I love you. But I can't do this anymore. I am done helping you find reasons to stay. It's killing me. So don't come to me about Mason anymore. I'm not going to help you stay anymore, but I'll help you leave whenever you're ready."

Boom.

Mason had successfully alienated me from my family and friends to the point that I rarely saw them. He was hostile or embarrassing when they came over, so they stopped coming over. And I rarely had the energy to be around anyone else, so I rarely went to them.

If I had called any of my friends or family, especially some of the men in my family who couldn't stand Mason, I'd have had an army show up to forcibly remove him. But I was too ashamed to ask.

Lynda was the last man standing. Pride never got in my way with her. So when I realized I was about to lose the only support system I had in place, it was a huge wake-up call.

The perfect storm had been brewing. Mason had dismantled every piece of me and burned my life to the ground, and I had given him the matches to do so. But Lynda's words, on top of the way Mason had escalated his carnage, did the trick.

That day, my forty-second birthday, when Mason called and I dropped the phone, Lynda's words played in my head. I knew I could not do one more day of him. I knew I would not make it through another crash without her there to pick me up, and I knew she'd be right there when I told her I was ready to leave this part of my life behind.

And she was.

Take a minute now to look around at your own life. Is there something or someone that you are holding on to even though it isn't good for you? Is there a relationship you are clinging to not because it is a healthy one or the one it used to be, but because you are hanging on to the illusion of what you want it to be, or what it used to be?

Is there a job that you hate, but you are staying in, and you complain about all the time?

Is there a habit that makes you sick, but you keep doing?

Is there a behavior that is holding you back, but you keep doing?

Is there someone you keep in your life because you feel responsible to them, even though they continue to hurt you?

What if you say to yourself, "I will no longer support you staying here, but I will do whatever it takes to support you leaving"?

It may feel silly at first, so if you need to say it in your head that's fine. But then move into saying it out loud. Write it on sticky notes and put it on your mirrors and your doors. Ask your friends to say it to you. Let it become your theme song to yourself, and then follow up on it.

I have spoken those words to myself countless times over the years, even if only to catch myself in a bad mood. Last night I got home from a long day and snapped at my fiancé and the animals because things were not put away and my son hadn't swept the dog fur off the stairs—stupid shit.

I bitched and moaned while I fed the dogs and stomped upstairs. I knew I was being an asshole and told myself I couldn't stop.

Dave said nothing to me. He just quietly got up and started straightening the kitchen.

The sight of this man, quietly absorbing the bitchiness he knew had nothing to do with some dishes in the sink and everything to do with my exhaustion and the pressure I was under, hit me hard.

I felt ashamed of myself for taking it out on him. I also, for a moment, felt powerless to leave my bad mood behind. But then I realized what Dave was doing in his own way.

He wasn't supporting my bitchiness by defending himself or snapping back at me. He was, instead, doing his best to help me feel better by removing the offensive mess. It was his way of shutting down a path to stay in a bad place and opening a path to a better place.

Sounds dumb, maybe, but I heard Lynda's words in his actions, and I was reminded again of how lucky I am to have people who stand strongly against my storms, from the light rains to the hurricanes.

The night flipped around immediately after that.

Who do you have in your life who refuses to fuel your negative moods while doing what they can to reconnect you with grace?

***

Terri and Lynda gifted me with their insight and support. I pull their words out often and apply them as needed in my life. I am lucky to have them as friends. I am also blessed to have met so many extraordinary people through our work with American Snippets. I've referenced some of those people throughout this book. One day I will begin a new series of topic-specific books that is entirely based on those interviews. For now, I'll share some of the best quotes on resilience our guests have left us with. Which one(s) resonates with you? If there is a quote that captures you, hop on to the AmericanSnippets.com website and catch that person's whole interview. Get the full experience, as many of our guests share things with us that they haven't before. Then find their websites and social media accounts and learn from them.

It is only by pushing past your fear that the healing and growth can be sustainable.

David Vobora

Some of the best comedy comes out of the darkest times.

Rob O'Neill

The full strength of the human spirit often lies in hiding until presented with something monumental.

Jason Schechterle

How you started is not how you have to finish.

Charlynda Scales

When success is a foregone conclusion, you can't lose.

Kent Clothier

WHAT NOT TO WEAR TO A MURDER TRIAL

The unconscious mind is where all the power is—it's where success and resilience is won or lost.

Michael Bernoff

Life is about pain and sacrifice and how we respond to it.

Larry Broughton

They say a bad beginning makes a good ending.

Major James Capers

Every little aspect of your life, you're either creating your empire or destroying it.

Elena Cardone

Humor is almost as important as faith because whatever has happened to you, if you can't find a way to laugh about it you're not going to make it through.

Taya Kyle

You have a choice in hard situations. Even if people feel sorry for you, you can choose not to. Instead you can choose positivity. You can choose the relentless mindset.

Jason Redman

What's it like to quit? I don't know because I never quit!

Ray Care

Chapter 12
Train Your Pain

They aren't sexy words, or magical ones. They sound pretty unsexy, in fact. But they represent the difference between those who are dominated by the power of their pain and those who harness that power for their own growth.

Post Traumatic Growth

I told you it doesn't sound very sexy. But when you dig into it, that changes.

Post Traumatic Growth, or PTG, is described as a transformation that follows a trauma. According to the American Psychological Association, Richard Tedeschi, PhD, and Lawrence Calhoun, PhD, developed this theory in the 1990s. Their theory states that a person who experiences a psychological struggle in the wake of trauma or adversity can experience positive growth. Tedeschi notes that "People develop new understandings of themselves, the world they live in, how to relate to other people, the kind of future they might have and a better understanding of how to live life," (Journal of Traumatic Stress, 1996).

They developed a Post Traumatic Growth Inventory. It is a list of five areas people develop growth in, following a trauma in their lives. Those areas are:

- Appreciation of life.
- Relationships with others.
- New possibilities in life.
- Personal strength.
- Spiritual change.

I discovered this information on PTG while I was researching my thesis. "Crime in the Military" was the title and I included information on several areas of trauma, including PTG. I thought at the time that PTG was something other people experienced. Not, I'm sure, someone who had suffered as much pain as I was constantly in. It must be nice for them, I thought.

It took several years for me to realize such growth is possible, and that I had achieved it myself. I had to go through a lot more pain before the lessons took hold but when they did, everything changed.

I can now tell you with confidence and 100% sincerity that PTG is real and it is, in fact, very nice.

Let's think of those five areas listed above as individual superpowers. We are born with them and we lose them all over time. Or at least, most of us lose most of them over time. We begin being told, "No." We hear people around us talk about the impossibilities and unfairness in life. We listen to the things people say about us. We get our hearts broken. We grow up and have bills to pay and bosses to answer to. We lose relationships and we encounter real life challenges that test our spirits.

Before we know it, we drive right past mountains and lakes that other people travel to see, and we don't even notice them anymore. We stop valuing the wonder of our hands and start taking that value for granted. We lose the gratitude for all the things we have and do and start obsessing on all the things we don't have or can't do.

Basically, we begin life with a free spirit and a limitless mindset, and then wind up living life with a burdened spirit and a scarcity mindset. As Dan Millman states in his book Way of the Peaceful Warrior, "The birth of the mind is the death of the senses."

For the first few years of our lives, we live only in the moment. We are fully present in those moments and we see wonder everywhere. Have you ever watched a baby discover their hands, for instance? Their absolute amazement as they stare intently at each finger and intentionally wiggle one at a time? When is the last time you stopped to appreciate the sheer wonder of your own hands? This hyper-awareness fades with each birthday until we become oblivious to most of our surroundings and ourselves.

Babies and young children have minds and hearts free of the clutter we carry as we get older. They eat, sleep, laugh, and cry whenever and wherever the moment feels right. They don't judge anyone other than by their own experiences. They don't care if you are white or black or old or young or rich or poor. They will stare with equal joy upon anyone who makes them laugh and equal fear at anyone who hurts them. They see right through our masks. This ability to receive the energy of people around them fades with age, too, as they learn to view people through specific lenses and clutter their minds with all the things that distract them.

Young children are in tune with themselves and the people around them in ways that are lost with age.

Do you remember when you were little and everything was possible, before people told you all the reasons why things are impossible? Do you remember when you moved into each day with nothing but anticipation about all the cool things you would do?

Do you wish you could feel that way again?

What would you do for that?

For now, focus on those feelings you are allowing to dominate your life. That pain that is currently having its way with you can be harnessed to discover and fulfill a potential you may not be able to envision right now, but which lies within us all.

Losing your sense of identity or your sense of purpose can be debilitating. It's enough to send some people into a downward spiral that takes years to reverse, if ever. For me, losing my identity as Lou's wife was debilitating. I loved being his wife and I was lost without that. Then losing my purpose of seeing his killer convicted and sentenced to death left me feeling like everything I'd done had been for nothing. I didn't know what to do with myself, and I spiraled further down.

Is there something in your life that you are so vested in that you'd be lost without? Is your career or your volunteer work or your hobby or your physical looks or abilities substantially attached to the identity you hold yourself together with?

Have you lost something that you based your identity or purpose on? What did you fill that void with? Did you manage to find a healthy way to fill that void, or are you still falling down into it? Are you propping yourself up on distractions or negative and unhealthy substitutes?

I've had the immense good fortune to meet hundreds of people who have crashed and burned physically, emotionally, professionally, and financially, and have painstakingly rebuilt their lives and rebranded their identities and purposes. They did so even though they struggled with things like suicidal tendencies or even failed suicide attempts. They did so in spite of unspeakable traumas and tragedies and failures and dangers. They built or rebuilt companies worth millions or hundreds of millions of dollars. They rebuilt broken and shattered bodies. They rebuilt broken or shattered minds and hearts.

I've shared some of those stories with you. Now let's learn from some more of these incredible people.

Trish Knudson loved being a police officer. She never felt uncomfortable in the male-dominated field as a female rookie. Instead, she slipped right into the camaraderie of the police force.

It was everything she could have hoped for and more, until tragedy struck.

Twenty-eight-year-old Marc Atkinson was a Marine Corps veteran, a husband, and new father. He was also one of Trish's close friends. One March night in 1999, she chatted and joked with Marc as usual before they went their separate ways. Less than an hour later, Trish responded to the call for an officer down and found herself desperately trying to revive life into her lifeless friend.

Marc had been ambushed and shot by drug dealers.

Trish and the rest of her brothers and sisters in blue were devastated. "It destroyed me," she remembers. It also redefined her as a police officer. Suddenly she was not so invincible. Suddenly she felt vulnerable. She even felt resentful.

"I'm thinking, we give our community everything we have every day, and this is what we get in return."

But just as quickly as that resentment began to take a grip on her, an outpouring of support from the community ripped that resentment right off.

Trish grappled with the weight of the trauma from that night and the loss of her dear friend. But with the enormous support from the community and a police department that went to extraordinary measures to step in and guide its officers through their pain, Trish found a new purpose in her job.

"It wasn't just a job anymore after his death. It was about Marc and not letting his death be in vain. It was about not ever having anyone in the community experience the hurt I felt when we lost Marc."

What helped Trish most through those dark times was identifying that her pain was bigger than anything she'd ever dealt with, and she needed help.

Asking for or accepting help was not a natural instinct for her. A childhood packed with loss and struggle had led her to build her own armor. She learned not to ask anyone for help. And now she was stuck— she knew she needed help but didn't know how to ask for it.

That's when the police department sent experienced SWAT officers to partner up with the police officers. Having a seasoned SWAT officer ride alongside her not only relieved the sense of vulnerability she'd been experiencing, but it also offered her a mentor in her grief.

"We had a badass sitting next to us," she says, one who reassured her that he'd been through what she was going through and came out stronger, so she could too.

"We get it," the SWAT officers reassured them all. "We will help you along on this ride. You are not going to walk this alone."

One of those SWAT officers especially connected with her. Today they are married. She smiles as she notes every situation can indeed have a silver lining.

It also opened her up to the drive to do even more with her life.

Dinner conversations with her husband quickly revealed that the job she'd once felt was as cool as could be was not winning the cool contest with her husband.

Trish's tolerance for pushing herself had been raised. She'd developed an increased capacity for pain and pushing herself that she could not lower back down. That energy and drive needed to be channeled somewhere positive.

The SWAT officers had left a strong impression on her. Hearing her husband talk about his job clicked it all into place for her, and Trish decided she wanted to be a SWAT officer as well.

Six months after she tested for SWAT she was placed on a team. Soon she was in the point cover position, which meant she was the second one to go through the door in dangerous situations. When the point position became open, Trish stepped into that role and was the first female Phoenix SWAT officer to lead the way through the door.

This was it. She was happily married and had the best job on earth, as far as she was concerned. She was an expert in her field, and she'd given her grief a purpose.

Life could not have been better until it got worse.

Tragedy reared back up in Trish's life. This time it aimed directly at her via the weapon in the hand of an armed suspect. It was a bad situation that had her twenty feet from the man. After hours of negotiation, the suspect fired.

Trish was struck in both legs. She fell to the ground amidst the chaos of the moment.

Although she recovered from her injuries, she was not able to recover enough to return to the career she loved.

Once again Trish's life was upended by tragedy. And once again Trish was ready to determine for herself what the purpose of her pain would be.

"It's about finding new meaning in your life," Trish says. Helping people was one of the biggest joys about her job. Trish accepted the fact that she was going to have to let her career go, but she was not about to let her whole purpose go with it. Instead, she found a new way to help people. "If I can't help people the way I'm used to," she asked herself, "how do I accomplish that in a different role?"

Today Trish not only shares her story with audiences, but she also teaches, trains, and consults on a variety of issues related to public safety. She instructs statewide for the Arizona Attorney General's Office on the topics of Street Medicine (Downed Officer) and Tactical Field Care. She's both a certified (AZPOST) firearms and general instructor.

She's presented multiple times on the Lessons Learned in Hostage Rescue for both the National Tactical Officers Association and the Arizona Tactical Officers Association, as well as spoken on additional police-related topics to various police departments and associations around the state and nation.

"I found new meaning by training people," says Trish.

The message Trish imparts to her audiences when she speaks is that help is out there and that no one has to walk their path alone. It's a lesson she resisted, but that changed everything for her.

Jeremy Harrell is another person who battled his way from Post Traumatic Stress to Post Traumatic Growth.

Jeremy signed on the dotted line for military service while he was still in high school.

Within a few years, he found himself on the first wave of combat deployments. The upside of being hands-on and directly helping besieged citizens in Iraq was exactly what he'd hoped it would be. The downside, however, was not.

The constant awareness that they were all in mortal danger took a toll on him. The experiences he had were not ones he could shake off. It was all "really detrimental to my mental health," he says, and more than the physical injuries he sustained, the mental and emotional ones caught him by surprise. Eventually the culmination of his measurable and immeasurable wounds meant he was deemed unfit for further service.

At first, Jeremy was bitter at the military for forcing him to accept a medical discharge.

He'd given this country a chunk of his youth and all of his inner peace. He'd seen things he could not unsee and had served with every ounce of strength he had.

Now that his body and mind were wounded, he was no longer of use? They'd used him up and spit him out? What was he supposed to do now?

His bitterness was the first of many things he'd have to overcome to build a new life for himself. It took him years to come to terms with it and even understand why the military needs to cut people like him loose.

Everyone he knew at home was getting married or climbing career ladders. Jeremy, on the other hand, was not even thirty years old and yet he felt like the best of his life was behind him.

He attempted to restart his civilian life with a career at UPS. It was during his time with that company that his true struggles were revealed to him.

One day it was the simple sight of an air tower near the office. The moment he laid eyes on it, he was filled with a rush of memories that broke him down right there in the parking lot. The reason?

It reminded him of how he'd felt each time he was in Kuwait. He'd stare at the air tower on base and realize how close he was to just hopping on a plane and getting out of the place he refers to as "the mecca of violence and death."

Another day it was the wake-up call from his boss, reminding him he was not in the military anymore and his leadership style needed to be adjusted accordingly. Jeremy hadn't even realized those who reported to him viewed him as unapproachable. He hadn't thought twice about dismissing requests to leave work or call in sick when employees didn't feel well. They were tired of his zero-tolerance policies and so was his own boss.

Then there was the insomnia. It was normal to him, but his friends didn't appreciate 3 a.m. phone calls. On and on it went, each day seeming to confirm to him that he no longer fit into the world he inhabited.

It was his wife who suggested the time had come for Jeremy to take actionable steps toward his own recovery. A horse enthusiast herself, she nudged Jeremy to inquire to a local equine therapy program.

More out of the need to placate his wife than out of genuine interest, Jeremy made the call. To his chagrin, he was accepted into the program and reluctantly made his first appearance in the barn shortly after.

It was the first day of the rest of his life.

From the moment he set foot in that barn, Jeremy felt an awakening he could not explain. His depression, hyper-vigilance, anxiety, anger—all of it disappeared in the presence of the horses. Their energy had a calming effect on him, and he made instant connections with his four-legged therapists.

He was smitten with all of it and there was no going back. Jeremy knew he'd not only found a way to directly overcome his own PTSD, but also a new purpose by helping other veterans do the same.

Today the once-reluctant equine therapy attendee heads his own nationally recognized program. The Kentucky Veterans Club uses equine therapy as its primary method of helping veterans through the same obstacles Jeremy once faced and must forever remain vigilant about. Cookouts, yoga, creative writing, and other recreational activities also offer opportunities for entire families to become connected.

Each event or activity looks on the surface to be strictly for fun, but underneath that fun is a mission being played out; veterans are connecting, unburdening themselves of the emotional toll of service, stretching physical limits they formerly operated under, and building relationships within their communities that turn into lifelong friendships and even a feeling of family.

The ultimate goal, says Jeremy, is to combat veteran suicide. The ripple effect is that it is also healing families and helping people move forward to enjoy life in the country they all gave so much for.

He smiles now as he remembers the bitterness he felt upon being discharged. Little did he know back then, he says, that it was in fact a blessing. "Learning to close one chapter and start another is difficult," he says, "but it can be done."

Trish and Jeremy both suffered from the impact of trauma, loss of purpose, and loss of identity. They both also dug deep within themselves to commit to rebuilding their purpose and identity in meaningful ways. Imagine if they'd just given up. Imagine if they'd allowed themselves to feed the victim mindsets instead of the victor. Imagine if they gave up on rebuilding anything in their lives because it was hard, and it even hurt sometimes.

Not only would they have missed out on all the wonderful moments that awaited them, but countless others would have never received the benefit of their impact. Think of the law enforcement officers who have connected with Trish and gained valuable skills from her expertise, or the audiences she fills with inspiration to carry back out into their lives. Think of the veterans and their families Jeremy's work has reached out and touched, of the marriages strengthened and the minds relieved and the hearts replenished.

Now think about your own pains, past and present. What has something you've overcome taught you about yourself or others or something in life? What is something you are experiencing right now going to be able to teach you if you are open to its lessons?

Have you lost a career you loved? What was it about that career you loved so much? How can you replicate that feeling or impact in another path? Has an injury or illness robbed you of the ability to do something you love? Apply the same question to that—how can you replicate the feeling you had doing that one thing, in another path?

The replication will not replace the loss. It won't erase the pain or absolve you of doing the work necessary to fully heal from your pain. It will, however, impact your own life in a positive way and quite possibly allow you to impact others.

You have a lot of wonderful moments ahead of you. Don't let your pain rob you of them.

Chapter 13
Power of Proximity

I cannot emphasize enough how important it is to protect your personal and professional space by defending it from those people and things that diminish those spaces. Then you must purify and add to that space by filling it with those people and things that fill your soul and your mind with creativity, positivity, and wisdom.

Where are you in your life, personally and professionally? Are you happy with exactly where you are right now, this minute, and the way your horizon looks if you keep the same people and the same habits as the major influencers in your life?

If the answer is Yes, you probably need to think about that again. Is there nothing left for you to aspire to, personally or professionally? Are you perfectly content with your fitness, finances, relationships, work, health, family, achievements, impact, surroundings, knowledge, wisdom, daily routine, vacations, and everything else?

I didn't think so. Otherwise, you wouldn't be reading this book.

Wanting to be more and do more with your life does not mean you aren't happy with your life or the people in it. It just means you want to be more and do more. The people in your life will either be a positive part of that path, a neutral part of that path, or a negative part of it.

The thing is, it's not up to them to decide that—it's up to you.

You can ask people in your life to support you, but you can't make them. Other than making that request, the power to change the people in your life is gone, so it's up to you to change the people in your life … or not.

Huh? What did she say, you ask?

It's been said before and I will say it again here: If you can't change the people in your life, then change the people in your life.

That's it. That's the major formula to design and build an inner circle that will be as valuable to you as you are to it.

If you want to travel the world but your spouse hates to travel and resents you for going alone and threatens to end your marriage if you go, you cannot blame your spouse for not fulfilling your dream if you accept those terms. If you make the decision to sacrifice one dream of traveling the world for the other dream of maintaining your marriage, that's on you.

Harsh, isn't it? But it's true, and the sooner you own your decisions the better. The sooner you understand the profound impact people can have on your life, the better. And the sooner you decide which relationships to keep, cut, or build based on how that relationship impacts you, the better.

Want to achieve something more with your life? Want to see more, do more, feel more, and live more than you are right now? Personal development, mental, emotional, and physical discipline, and all the mindset work in the world will not be enough if you allow people in your life to have a greater negative impact on you than the positive impact you have on yourself.

The power of your proximity is immense. Who are you most influenced by, both directly and indirectly? Who are the people in your everyday life? Who do you learn from, look up to, emulate, and connect with? Are they working with you on your path? Are they working against you, or are they indifferent?

The best way to maximize your inner circle is to diligently build it. Triage the people in it and the time you spend with them. Do the same for your personal habits.

There is a system I created for triaging the people and habits in your life. It is a simple-to-understand system that can be difficult to do, as we tend to be hesitant about changing our relationships and habits. But I got you covered and can help you through.

I teach this system in workshops or one-on-one coaching. Whenever someone applies this and sticks to it, they see a shift in their own lives. I love it!

In order to make this work for you, you have to allow yourself to focus on you. There is a time and a place to help others, but you cannot pour from an empty cup. When you achieve wealth, you can donate more to others. When you achieve fitness, you can train others. When you achieve personal fulfillment, you have more energy to offer others.

So for this chapter, focus on strengthening yourself just like you have in the other chapters.

Ready?

Write down some goals you have—lose weight, drink less, exercise more, learn something, ace a test, get a promotion, get a job, meet someone special, make your first million or your hundredth million, etc. There is no set rule for this part. You can focus on one major goal, write a list of several goals, or get really creative and write out a highly detailed description of what a perfect day would look like for you when you achieve all those things you dream of. Have fun with this part—go big!

Once you've got that done, the work begins.

Make another list—this one will be big. List the people you see every day. Then list the people you have contact with on a regular or daily basis. This can be in person or online or through an app, whatever. Then list the people you may not have frequent contact with but who play a role in your life.

Got that done? Go back and check it again. Did you forget someone?

Then use this guide to rank each person or item from 0–3:

0 = criticizes/talks down/talks against that goal or your ability to achieve it

1 = does not express either objections or support; is neutral, unconcerned with that goal

2 = expresses support and encouragement for that goal but does not follow that up with tangible support (does not share your social media posts, refer you to others, offer to help, etc.)

3 = offers tangible support or advice toward helping you meet that goal

Next, rank each person from 0–3 again.

0 = models the opposite of my goal; states goals but spends more time complaining than focusing on solutions to challenges (e.g., your goal is to focus on your health and wellness and this person is committed to unhealthy habits like binge drinking, overeating, incessant complaining, etc.)

1 = professional victim; full of reasons life is unfair and excuses for not doing more with their own life

2 = states goals and works to achieve them, but tends to give up before reaching those goals

3 = exemplifies a commitment to a goal, has reached one or more significant goals in their life, and encourages and supports you on your path

Now do the math. Add the score up for each person. What do the scores tell you?

6 = rock stars in your life; they are your champions

5 = somewhat strong supporter and positive influence

4 = smack dab in the middle of supporting and not supporting you

3 = less supportive of you; may sometimes be helpful but can't be counted on for help

2 = barely supportive of you; will not be helpful

1 = not supportive of your goal and will not be helpful to you in reaching it

0 = not supportive at all; will hinder your progress

On a separate piece of paper, make another list. Yes, really. You've come this far, what's the point of quitting now? I bet you can finish this whole thing in less time than you spend on Pinterest or whatever your virtual addiction is.

So this next list will be the content you consume. What podcasts do you listen to? What social media sites do you spend your time on? What apps do you use? What books do you read, what movies do you watch, what shows do you binge, etc.? Don't skimp on this. You are the only person who will see it unless you are moved to share it. Now is not the time to deny that you watch every episode of The Bachelor and chat live with your friends while you do so. We all have our indulgences.

Rank each item on that list from 1–5, with 1 being the least impactful on helping you reach your goals and 5 being the most impactful. While you're at it, write down how much time per day you direct your energy toward each item.

I know you know what comes next, but I'll say it anyway.

Once you have the people and things in your life classified, it's time to trim the fat. Get rid of the people and things that do not bring value to your emotional, physical, mental, or financial version of success.

If that sounds cold, ask yourself why?

Why feel like you have to light yourself on fire to keep someone else warm?

There is a difference between being compassionate and being a doormat.

Look deeply at the relationships in question and separate the two in order to know who to cut and who to keep, if even on a reframed structure.

If you are not just interested in your own success, but invested in it, you will see this part through. Before you move on to this next step, go back and make sure you didn't rush through the previous steps. Don't let yourself feel bad for assigning someone a low score. It doesn't mean you're a bad person or that they are either. It just means in terms of the goals you have for yourself, that person is not an asset.

I'll focus on the low scorers first, to alleviate some of the resistance or fear attached.

A low-scoring person or habit does not necessarily mean you have to remove that person or thing from your life entirely. Unless someone is actively sabotaging you, it is possible to keep them in your life and still achieve your goals, if you minimize your exposure and absolutely compartmentalize any negative energy they emit so it does not reach the space you are nurturing positivity in.

If you are trying to lower your cholesterol and your friends keep ordering French fries for lunch, you don't have to avoid them at lunch, but you do need to mentally brace yourself to withstand the temptation they are placing before you.

I have people in my life I genuinely like, respect, and enjoy spending time with. But their paths are different from mine, and mine is different from theirs, so we rarely overlap now that our kids are all grown. When we do get together on those rare occasions, we have a few hours of fun catching up on one another's kids and lives without really having much in common in terms of our goals and visions. No one I know in my day-to-day physical proximity has written a book, for instance. No one is working on writing one either. So while I write my books, I don't turn to them to brainstorm publishers and covers and marketing. And while they work on their careers as teachers or nurses or landscapers or whatever, they don't brainstorm with me on their professions.

We are all probably a 3 or a 4 score in each other's lives not because we don't like one another, but because our interests and aspirations are different. So we naturally limit our time together while enjoying the times we do get together.

Sometimes we cannot cut a person out of our life, especially if they are family. Maybe it's a coworker you can't avoid seeing, or a relative that's at every family gathering, etc. Removing every negative obstacle is not the goal. Removing their impact from you is. So if you cannot avoid something or someone that works against your well-being, allow yourself to remove any impact they have on you. Just dismiss their credibility and, rather than absorb any of the negativity they emit, deflect it as being more about them than you.

That being said, the more 5- and 6-ranked people in your life, the better. Every number below that is dead weight in terms of your goals. On the other side, if you expect the 5- and 6-ranked people in your life to allow you in their circle, you better strive to be a 7 in theirs. This works both ways. Don't expect someone who is committed to creating their own version of fulfillment to spend too much time with you if you are not up to the level where you help them move that needle forward. It doesn't mean they don't like you as a person. It just means they can't add your weight to their climb. They will encourage you, and when they reach the top they will likely turn around and offer you a hand, but don't expect them to slow their climb for you any more than you want to slow yours for someone else. There is a limit to the weight a person can carry without abandoning their own climb. Learn how to balance the weight you carry for others with the rate of your own expectations for your own climb too.

It feels good to help other people, just like it's critical to receive help. Understanding the difference between positive help and negative help is key.

Need some more help figuring out the people in your life?

Think back to some of your happiest moments and biggest achievements. Then think back to the worst moments and biggest disasters. Who was with you? Who had access to your mindset? Who was running your decisions— was it you alone, or were there other people involved? What was the level of their involvement and is that something you wish to repeat?

That should help.

Sometimes, making several circles is helpful. Make one circle for your professional goals, another for your family goals, and another for your socialization or recreational ones. This allows you to feel less trepidation about keeping certain people out of one central circle. Once you've trimmed some fat, you may realize your circle is pretty empty. That's okay—small, tight-knit circles are powerful. But if there is a gap— someone who could inspire you to do one thing or teach you how to do another—fill it!

Back to the mentorship topic: remember how I found Terri Seifert to help prepare for the court martial? What is it in your life that you would like to learn about to be better poised to overcome or achieve it?

Find the people in that space and study them. Pay for a mastermind or individual coaching. Invest your time and resources to build a relationship with those people and learn how to provide value to them, and you will have solved the riddles before you in that area while expanding your network.

Whether you want to make more friends, learn how to build an engine, learn how to start a company, raise capital, heal from grief, run for office, write a book, cook, or anything else, there is a mentor for you. There are resources for you. The more you are willing to invest your time and money to connect to those resources, the more direct and impactful your education will be.

I've invested thousands of dollars for masterminds, coaching, and events. I have not regretted a single dime, because each experience helped me elevate my game.

You are investing right now. You invested money to buy this book and the time to read it. What are you going to do with those investments? Are you going to get a return on them, or are you going to just write it off as another time-filler?

Chapter 14
Why to Woo a Widow

I practically ran down the aisle to marry Lou. I was twenty-three years old and the world lay before us to conquer. For nine-and-a-half years, I lived the gift of being his wife. Now I have walked through more wedding anniversaries without him than with him.

A lot has changed.

On my left hand, I'm wearing another man's ring, and I'll soon be his wife. I love this ring and I love this man, just as fiercely as I love Lou and will always hold on to that part of my heart.

This ring symbolizes the new life I almost prevented myself from finding. It is simple and unpretentious and precise in its purpose.

On my right wrist, I wear a black memorial bracelet with Lou's name and the date of the tragedy that stole him from us.

It is a beautiful balance.

When I look at my left hand, I see all life still holds. I see the man who understands me and possesses the confidence, grace, tenacity, and humor that enable him to love all of me and commit to spending his life alongside me. I am excited for our future, and I love each day with him.

When I look at my right wrist, I pause the whirlwind around me. I remember that the majority of what has me worried is, in the grand scheme, irrelevant. I remind myself of how none of that mattered one single bit after Lou died, and how I regret the time wasted being worried instead of living in that moment with him.

On my left hand is a reminder that life is a gift and happiness is a choice. I could have given up dozens of times. I paid deeply for misplacing my trust and hiding from my pain instead of facing it. I could have let myself believe I don't deserve this second chance and walked away from the possibility. But I didn't, and here he is.

On my right wrist is a reminder that there will one day be an extraordinarily cruel price to pay for this new love. Indeed, the decision to allow myself to feel it makes me once again vulnerable to the agony of it being taken from me—or he will feel that agony. I don't know which outcome I most dread. Sometimes, this knowledge paralyzes me.

On my left hand is the evidence of my decision to accept this cost. This time I am not going to squander one single moment away. This time, I recognize every decision to waste a moment or to savor it and choose to savor them all, regardless of what they may be. I also take responsibility for ensuring that, should he be the one to experience grief when I am gone, I will have done all I can to ensure he doesn't regret the cost.

I loved once, with every fiber of my being. Then I lost that, and the power of that love was turned against me with a venom that nearly destroyed me. I felt betrayed, punished by love.

Now, I use that lesson as a way to maintain perspective.

There is a great temptation to let shame dominate my heart when I look back at the two disastrous relationships I got myself into, not to mention the, um, other moments that took place on my path to love after loss. But each time shame sweeps into my heart, I forcefully kick it right back out. Sometimes I turn back to Elaine's words to free myself from that shame and the guilt that accompanies it.

I was just doing my best with what I had at the time. My resiliency, confidence, and perspective were not in place. That's the beauty of it all, isn't it—the way we grow.

Part of my path to forgiving myself and extracting lessons from my experiences has been to dig deep into not only myself but the whole widow thing.

If I couldn't figure out why someone should entrust me with his heart, broken but beautiful as it was, how was I supposed to expect anyone else to? That's when I really dialed in the whole thing. Just like the stages of grief, there are stages of growth through grief. The goal is to reach the stage of Post Traumatic Growth as discussed in the previous chapter.

Dave got a lot of questions from concerned family and friends. How was he able to love a widow whose husband was murdered and who went through that trial and was always going to be attached to that in some way? Was he sure he wanted to attach himself to all that baggage and drama?

All fair questions. Dave figured out the answers as we went. He was just following his own heart. It would be awesome to have a guide for anyone wary about wooing a widow, wouldn't it? Just as important is a guide for widows to check in with themselves before taking that plunge again.

I wish I'd had a better understanding of it all back then. Now that I do, here's what I discovered:

At first blush, it probably seems like falling in love with a widow (or a widower, but I'll keep it simple here) is a terrible idea. I mean, why would you want to strap that baggage to your back, right?

Whether she's young or old or in between, she's probably a straight-up hot mess, don't you think? You could never live up to the memory of a man who has been sanitized to the level of sainthood, could you? Why would you even want to try—who needs to deal with in-laws at all, let alone in-laws of the man whose wife you're sleeping with?

The pictures in the house, the bouts of grief for the love she lost, on and on that list grows until it does in fact appear that only the most masochistic man alive would ever volunteer for that shit show.

Unless she's got a nice big inheritance or life insurance policy, anyway.

But what if I let you in on something that can potentially lead you to the greatest love you will ever know? Would you be interested in that?

A person who has experienced the enormity of grief knows exactly what she is risking when she opens her heart back up to love. There is no more illusion that death will happen "one day" or the blissful ignorance of what that particular hell feels like. If she still chooses to love again despite that, she is a warrior. If she has done the agonizing work of healing her heart, understanding how to manage the grief that will always be present, and readying herself to accept that she may very well experience that loss again, she is a gem.

Imagine a relationship with someone who has an enhanced awareness of her blessings. She has a greater appreciation of life and for relationships. She is aware of an innate strength she has that can carry her through struggles she once would have buckled under. She will gladly extend that strength to you. She sees possibilities everywhere and she has a spiritual foundation that is both unique to her and is unbreakable.

This does not mean she is perfect. It's called post traumatic growth, not perfect traumatic growth.

She will still have annoying habits and do stupid shit. But she will also learn from her mistakes and be quick to forgive you yours. She simply will not waste energy on the petty things she once allowed to ruin a day or a moment.

A person who has achieved post traumatic growth will absorb life's hits and separate those that truly matter from those that do not. She will still struggle with some of those hits, but she will have learned how to recognize those struggles she can navigate alone and those she needs help with.

In case you missed the importance of that last part, I'm going to break it down.

Understanding when to ask for help and having the strength to do so is HUGE.

It takes more strength and humility to admit we need help, and then ask for it, than it does to allow stubbornness and false pride prevent us from asking.

I'm not talking about the kind of help that goes along with being lazy or playing a professional victim. I'm talking about the kind of help you need to move forward past a real place of pain, or a professional hurdle, or any area you are stuck in, and working to get out of.

Imagine being in a relationship with someone who handles much of life's daily challenges on her own but who also comes to you when she truly needs your help. Imagine her appreciating you being there for her instead of taking your help for granted.

She will hold herself accountable for her own happiness, and you for yours, but she will find happiness in the smallest of moments.

Even while she's barking at you for flooding the bathroom floor every time you shower, she'll be savoring the way it annoys her, because she knows it's something she will give anything to complain about again if she loses you.

When you roll with the way she isolates herself sometimes, she will love you harder for understanding her need to do so.

You will know that she expects you to make every single moment matter in your life even if she's taken from you. And you will know that however broken she may be if she loses you first, she will still find her way to savor beauty again.

On the other hand, a woman who has been through a few different layers of hell and found her way out the other side will be quick to cut herself loose from anyone who tries to pull her back there. If you find her strength and confidence sexy when you meet her, woe be it to you if you change your mind about that later. If you aren't confident and strong yourself, you will resent those very things about her once it becomes clear she's not going to drive below the speed limit just because you don't want to keep up with her.

You will see her taillights disappear over the horizon, and she won't be looking back in her rear view for you.

Unfortunately, many a widow attempts to fly from her nest of grief too soon, only to freefall down into a massive splat. She hasn't matured through her grief enough. She hasn't given her wings time to grow, and she hasn't learned how to ride the currents.

I know this all too well.

My first relationship with my neighbor Keith was doomed from the start. No surprise there. But then I got cocky and told myself I'd reached all these new levels of growth and perspective and was genuinely ready to be trusted with another shot at flight. That led me to Mason.

I've already shared that disaster with you as well.

There are men like Mason who will woo a widow just like he'd woo any woman that he senses he can prey on. Trust, vulnerability, and a good heart in a widow is just as good as in anyone else. More so, perhaps, because there are so many other emotional angles to exploit. A predator is a predator, and prey is prey.

Then there are the knights. These are the guys who are drawn to the poignancy of a widow's love, and whose overdeveloped sense of masculinity responds to the notion of being that knight in shining armor who swoops in like the hero he is and rescues the damsel in distress. His protective nature doesn't end there though. Instead, he will seek to be needed every day. He will need to be needed, actually, and if the widow matures in her grief, finds her own strength, and begins to evolve into someone who no longer feels like she needs to be rescued from herself or life or anyone else, conflict will arise.

Knights and predators are different: the predator knows he's a predator and loves it. The knight often has sincere intentions and believes he is doing what's best. It's only when that belief is challenged that he either recognizes the truth and does the work to evolve himself past that or becomes defensive about it because he's not ready to admit he has his own issues that need to be addressed.

I know many, many widows who have been wooed by knights and predators, including myself. It's hard to see these stories repeated in the grief groups I've been a part of for years. If we went solely on those experiences, we may believe that it's pretty impossible to find true love a second time around. We may believe that a widow is unlikely to be wooed by anyone with the mindset, heart, confidence, and sense of adventure required to both respect and appreciate her as much for what she's lost as for what she's become.

Fortunately, there is another kind of man who will woo a widow.

He's the man who didn't seek a widow out but who does not turn and run at the news. He instead approaches her with an open mind. Perhaps he's been widowed himself, or perhaps he's been through his own version of trauma or pain that gives him an awareness of the strength it takes to put yourself out there again. Or maybe he's just a good guy who has not gone through anything truly terrible in life but possesses the traits to roll it all into his love for her.

I love seeing those stories appear in the grief groups, and I love that I have my own.

So let's now take a trip through the fun side of love after loss. My hope is that my love story gives its own hope to you, if you are convinced you don't deserve another dance in the sun. Or, if you are happily dancing right now, let this next chapter bring you back to your own story of meeting your love, and the broken road that led you to him.

Chapter 15
Love After Loss

Maybe a smarter person would have given up on love after the disastrous impact I'd allowed Mason to have on us. In some ways I think I did give up, at least as far as finding another soulmate or deep, true love. But through the months of introspection and rebuilding my life, I realized that I still wanted to get out there and live. I didn't feel like I needed a relationship. I just wanted to keep the channels open to maybe developing one someday. In the meantime, I figured it would be nice to find someone to hang out with, laugh with, and play with on occasions. I'd never casually dated before. It seemed like a good time to try it out.

Besides, hadn't I just spent months teaching myself how to be courageous and remain invested in finding all the joy life still has to offer? Wouldn't I be failing myself if I didn't give it a shot now that I was wiser?

I was in my early forties at that point. I knew if I waited until I was fifty or sixty to get back out there, I'd probably never try at all. So back into the arena I went.

You can get anything online. Even love, if you know how to shop for it. My approach may not be for everyone, but it worked for me. I figured if I am going to expect complete honesty from a man and be as efficient as possible in terms of time and energy wading through the bullshitters, I should probably cull the herd right off the bat.

So I crafted a profile write-up that served as its own gauntlet. Any man who took the time to read the whole thing already showed some follow-through. That's a plus. Any man who read the whole thing and still pinged me could not say he wasn't warned, and any man who pinged me but showed no evidence that he'd read it at all was instantly dismissed.

Not a bad starting point. Better to have no potential matches, I knew, than to have dozens of false ones.

If you were a man on Match.com or eharmony.com back then, maybe you saw this profile:

Greetings Matchelors.

I have experienced the absolute worst of humanity but been helped through tough times by the absolute best. Now I have finally hit my stride and decided to take another shot at finding what I once had, again.

I'm a widow, but not a cougar widow. So as entertaining as lines like, "If you were younger, I'd take you for a ride," may be, please, please, please—spare me. I don't hold it against you. I'm not exactly slaying the nuances of the dating world either. This is largely because I am not versed in the art of being coy; if I like you, I actually tell you I like you. If I think I sense potential, I will say so. In my mind this means … "I like you, and I would like to focus on just you for now." But I am sensing in your mind it may translate to, "We should declare our undying love for each other, and wear matching outfits to Christmas dinner."

Um … no.

On the flip side, if I don't get that vibe, I'm out. Whether we've had a few dates or have never met, if I feel like it's not right, I will say so too. Because I think you deserve the truth, and I hope you do the same. I'm a big girl and I have survived far worse than dead-end dating. Although it is a close second.

Ha.

This seems like common sense to me, but then again, I suck at this.

Before I forget—the people with no pictures viewing or winking at me—you're creeping me out. It's weird to be hit on by a phantom. Stop it. Ditto if your profile pic looks like the Unabomber, or if there is a chance I could bump into your parents at my high school reunion. But, if you live within reasonable driving distance, are fit, funny, and have your shit together, we could at least make it through a meeting for drinks.

End of that section.

There was another part to a profile where you could add a short summary. Some people didn't bother. But I did:

A little about me—I am a mom, and my boys are my priority. But moms need a life too, and my kids don't mind getting rid of me sometimes. I have too many dogs. I work, manage to hold my life together, and can not only dish heaping portions of sarcasm, but I can take it, too. I can be intense. I love to be playful. I have to get outside. Dressing up for a swanky night out is fun and I can still rock a cocktail dress on a good night, but jeans and cowboy boots are my usual attire. I can absolutely outride you on a mechanical bull, and I dare you to try to beat me. Extra points to a man who knows his way around a horse, understands the value of candlelight, and has an overall appreciation of life, challenges and all.

As trust grows, so does intimacy. Patience is required, but so worth it. Easing into this pool rather than diving in. Admittedly a wee bit jaded but still not ready to admit defeat.

A little about who I hope to meet—he will be as mentally and emotionally stable as any of you can be (yes, that was a little sarcastic). He will be financially stable, fun, quick to laugh and confident enough to tempt me into meeting without being cocky. He will be witty but not obnoxious, and will be physically fit and adventurous. Enjoys a day of hiking but not afraid to clean up and go out on occasion.

I sound like an absolute package, right?

Here's the real truth behind that profile: I told myself I was being honest for all the responsible reasons. But really, I intentionally layered it on to self-sabotage the process. I did know I wanted to find love again, but I was also beginning to believe I'd already had my dance in the sun, and that was my only dance. Part of me was also afraid to be hurt again, not by someone I love dying, but by someone being an asshole. I figured if I put that profile out there, I could at least tell myself I was brave enough to take another chance while never really taking the chance.

That all changed when a few men decided to run the gauntlet.

Dave was a late arrival. By the time I saw him, I was juggling a few different Matchelors and going through the process of elimination. Not just on my side, mind you; they were all going through their own process and some of them eliminated me from their lineups too.

I feel sorry for the dude named Lou who sent me a message …

Dating is its own discipline. I never dated before Lou. He was my first real boyfriend, aside from the teenage train wreck experience in high school. I had four kids to raise and a full-time job about to start. I didn't really have time to waste. I also wasn't about to let myself be preyed upon again, so I enlisted two of my besties to be on a selection committee. All candidates went through their scrutiny. Jenn and Lynda got screenshots of their pictures and bios, and updates on the messages.

We had fun with it.

Once a candidate met their approval, he was cleared for a meeting. I made sure not to exclude a candidate if he didn't look like my type. Instead I went for personality, knowing that the true test would be the energy felt when we met.

Energy did its work quickly. One by one I crossed them off, sometimes after trying hard to find that zing because someone was so sweet, or hot, or fun. But without that spark there's no point, so onward I went.

My committee and I gave them nicknames like Marine Mark and Martial Arts Guy. Those two were the front runners even though I knew on some level they were long shots. Still, the committee approved and understood I needed to have some fun in the process, so they granted me some play passes.

On paper, Marine Mark was a great catch. A veteran of, you guessed it, the Marines, he had a solid job, sizable income, grown kids, and wanted to find a woman to travel with. The fact that I couldn't exactly leave four boys home to travel with anyone, let alone a man I barely knew, didn't seem to register with him.

His texts were funny and the laugh factor is what kept me on the hook. But the few dates we had went from uncomfortable to warning lights flashing in my brain pretty quickly. The last straw was memorable:

Marine Mark talked me into meeting him out for dinner after I'd already eaten with the kids. He even made the hour drive to meet me near my home. By the time I arrived at the restaurant, I was actually dreading his hello kiss. I knew that meant it was time to end this road.

There he was, all six-foot-something of him, flashing a smile and looking like the man he sounded like in texts. But then he spoke, and I was already looking forward to leaving. The comment about driving out to see me being worth something more than the quick kiss could have been light and playful from someone else, but his tone suggested otherwise.

166

It didn't get better inside. Who orders pickled baby octopus—ever—let alone on a date?

Marine Mark does.

So not only was I dodging the smell and the sight of the bright pink baby octopi wiggling like Jell-O on his fork, but I also had to do that while hearing Marine Mark talk about … Marine Mark. He told me all the reasons he dumped other women. He told me about the trip to Mexico he wanted me to take with him. He'd even pay for it as long as I understood we would be sharing a room and that came with certain expectations.

Finally I had enough. I had to go, I told him, and that's when it happened.

Marine Mark leaned forward as if to tell me a secret. Trying to be polite, I leaned in to humor him—and he blew in my face. Not like a soft puff, either. More like blowing out birthday candles.

The look of disgust on my face was hilarious to him. That, he said, was just to prepare me for the octopus breath I'd experience when I gave him my pathetic kiss goodnight and ran home to my kids.

I didn't bother making him walk me out to my car.

The committee was appropriately offended and amused at the same time. None of us had high hopes for Marine Mark, anyway.

About this time, I noticed another guy on both Match.com and eharmony.com. "HoneyBrown" wasn't someone I'd say looked like my type but then again, if pressed, I could never really explain what my type was. That's because I base my type on energy. When I reflected on that, I realized this guy did indeed fit my type.

We checked each other out a few times before he sent me a message. He was polite, confident, funny, and interested. Check, check, check, and check! He appeared to have his own business, he had two young kids, and he loved his dog. The committee loved him.

The problem was, I had too many active candidates already. This guy seemed like he was too nice for me. As in, I didn't want him to waste his time on me when I was already feeling overwhelmed with the process and considering taking a break from it all. Dating different men was not my style, and it was getting old. I still had three or four guys to sort out and if none of those clicked with potential, I was going to step away for a bit.

There was also MAG.

Martial Arts Guy was another committee favorite. We'd been messaging for a couple weeks and graduated to phone calls and texts. He was hysterical. I always looked forward to hearing from him. He was also a single father. His daughter's picture was adorable, and he clearly doted on her. Did I mention he owned his own martial arts company?

I wasn't sure where the potential was with MAG, but the back-and-forth with him was becoming something I didn't want to stop. Then came the night my kids all slept at their grandparents', and I went to a committee meeting at my friend's house. We laughed and had fun with the messaging on Match.com. The messaging process had become so predictable with so many of the men who were there strictly for hook-ups that I knew exactly how to get them to say certain things. We made a drinking game out of it. Each time I told them a word or phrase I'd get the guy to say, and he said it, the committee had to drink.

In the midst of this, MAG texted me. (Trevor, Colin, Sean, and Jeremy—you may want to skip this part. Mom, you should sit this out, too.)

I was not exactly under the influence of alcohol, but I was also not exactly under the influence of common sense, either. Before I knew it, MAG was on his way over for our first in-person meeting.

Being as I really had no idea about the nuances of dating, I had no clue that night took me out of the "relationship potential" category and placed me firmly in the "use this chick to blow off steam while I spend time getting to know the other chick that I'm really interested in" category.

MAG showed up and I guess I'd just made my first booty call (sorry mom, I told you not to read this, and to my kids—I told you to skip this part too).

It was a unique experience for me. I didn't really feel good about it, but I didn't feel too bad either. It was all part of the process, I told myself.

MAG followed up by inviting me to his place the following week. I told "HoneyBrown," whose name I'd learned is Dave Brown, that as much as he seemed like a great guy, I was figuring things out with someone and I didn't feel right going out with him in that process. To me, doing dinner or drinks with different guys was one thing, but if I was intimate with one man, I was not going to be exploring a relationship with another.

MAG, on the other hand, was apparently thinking the opposite, and giving himself time to explore another relationship while using me to help him be patient about intimacy with the woman who he actually respected.

Live and learn.

I spent a couple months driving an hour to his house once a week, while my kids were in school. Each time I told myself the hours we spent together were showing signs of potential to actually go out on a date, meet his friends, or do something other than breakfast, play time, and a rerun of Sons of Anarchy. Not that I didn't enjoy any of that, but breakfast was more satisfying than play time for me, because he was not really interested in my side of things. And I'd already watched the entire Sons of Anarchy series, so I knew what happened to whom.

As the weeks wore on, Dave and I would occasionally message. He'd told me more about himself, and I resisted the pull I felt toward him because I was already in this thing with MAG and felt like I had to play it out.

"Are you ready to stop messing around with those other guys yet?" Dave would ask, and I'd reply, "Almost." Then he'd wish me a good week and remind me I could message him whenever I wanted.

Gradually the committee and I sorted through candidates and narrowed it down to MAG and Dave. This was the result of more than a few colossally awkward moments, bad dates, or having that work done for us when someone else dumped, rejected, or ghosted on me. I couldn't help but feel like there was something special about Dave, and yet I was still going to MAG's house once a week.

The situation with MAG was unraveling, though. My attempts to lure him to my house, or out in public, were met with resistance. The one time he humored me, he was open about not wanting to bump into anyone he knew.

Just when I would be ready to give up, he'd say something funny or we'd have some sort of moment where it felt like he was more than just using me. But after a few more weeks went by, and we'd circled the drain a few times, the day came when it all blew up.

I'd tell you how I showed up at his house on the usual day, but I have to spare myself some humiliation.

Let's just say he was less than happy to see me that day. We'd apparently miscommunicated the night before, so he didn't think I was coming. By the time he answered his door, I was pissed, and he wasn't even pretending to be glad to see me.

"You may as well come in," he said, "and I'll make some breakfast anyway."

The weeks of setting my pride aside were over. I'd recognized the old habit I'd defaulted back to, of putting my own feelings and sense of self-worth aside to please someone else. Just like all the other times I'd done it, this had been received not so much with gratitude but with cockiness. The more I humbled myself for him, the more he knew I was a doormat he could walk all over. And since I not only allowed it to happen but made it easy for him, who could blame him for doing so, really?

That day, though, I hit a new awareness of the cycle I had allowed myself to be pulled back into. MAG wasn't a bad guy, but he was a guy who was clearly just using me, had no real respect for me, and no intent of ever getting to know me better. I was a convenience for him, nothing more. I didn't stay for breakfast, or anything else. He didn't try to stop me.

Well, I thought, as I drove home biting back humiliated tears and waves of self-loathing, that was that. I was still pissed though. I needed to be able to pretend I ended this on my terms, not his. So I pulled over and sent him a text noting that it was clear we weren't going anywhere and wishing him well.

He responded as if confused over why I'd been so annoyed and left, but he agreed that we'd run our course.

I'm not sure what I'd expected, but apparently that wasn't it. I took my anger out on the back road, noting how even the dreary winter sky wasn't pretending to shine any light on the moment.

You know what? I asked myself. *You deserve better than this. Better to be single forever than to ever let anyone make you feel like that again. Time for you to really take control of your own drive.*

The next two things I did were game changers.

First, I sent one more text to MAG. The exact wording escapes me, but it went something like, "Actually, MAG, you've been kind of an asshole to me, and I can't blame you because I let you. So while I still wish you well, I have to get some kind of win here." I then went on to spoil the entire series of Sons of Anarchy for him. I told him who gets killed by whom, when it happens, and how it all ends in the very last episode.

Mind you, MAG was hooked on this series, and watching it was something he really looked forward to. This was almost as screwed up of me to do as a good-old-fashioned car-keying, and I knew it.

It didn't take long for my phone to buzz and confirm I'd landed a significant blow. He was not happy with me. He was far more upset that I'd ruined Sons of Anarchy for him than that our weekly meetups were over.

This filled me with a petty kind of joy.

It also made me determined to turn this shitty situation into a win.

"Okay, you're up," I texted Dave. "Let's meet tomorrow night."

Part of me didn't like this cocky version of me that came out around Dave. Another part of me loved it. I didn't know how he'd respond, but he'd been so cool for weeks now, making me laugh, getting some sarcastic jabs in at me, teasing me about how he'd take me out for a candlelight mechanical bull ride one night, that I gambled he'd see through the arrogance for more good-natured playfulness.

"Good," he said, "I was getting tired of waiting behind this velvet rope."

And just like that he had me.

Dave rearranged his weekend schedule to meet me the following night. We settled on the Texas Roadhouse in a town near me. Casual but energetic, conveniently located for a quick getaway, and home of delicious fried pickles.

171

I saw him as soon as I walked through the door. He hadn't doctored any pictures or fudged any info on his appearance. He looked exactly like he was supposed to. I had a few seconds to check him out before he picked his head up from his phone and saw me.

Here's where it gets cheesy, but you can take it.

When his eyes caught mine and he smiled at me, it didn't feel like I was meeting someone new. It felt like I was being reunited with someone I missed. It was like a voice inside me wanted to yell to him, "There you are!"

There was no awkwardness, no stalled conversations, no annoyed look when I explained to him that my phone was remaining on the table in case my kids called me for anything. He understood that because he is a dad. He even respected it.

The only time I was nervous the entire night was when I realized how strong of a connection I felt to him. It freaked me out, actually, to the point I began fixating on every detail of him in order to find some sort of flaw that would be enough to override that connection.

This whole experience of dating had been done only half-heartedly. I'd known MAG and Marine Mark and the others were not going to be my next great loves. But I wanted the comfort of telling myself that at least I'd tried. I was about to start a full-time job and the days of meeting someone for coffee or lunch while the boys were in school were over. Dave was going to be the last guy I met before letting Jesus take the wheel.

Little did I know, Jesus had been driving the whole time.

That first good night kiss is something we laugh about still. I was hesitant to go all-in and leery of him pushing himself on me. The polite, soft, quick kiss he gave me was another big check mark in my book. It left me wanting more, and looking forward to that, rather than feeling like I'd just been violated.

It wasn't until over a year later when I told him he'd given me the perfect first kiss that he revealed he'd been as turned off by my stiffness as I'd been turned on by his restraint.

Real life is not a fairy tale.

Our next date was in his town, about an hour from my place (the distance was a good thing in my mind—it would help keep this casual). He took me to a nice restaurant, ordered us the Couple's Dish for two, and proceeded to eat pretty much the whole thing himself. I wasn't making it hard for him to eat the meat—it was raw and bloody and disgusting. The potatoes, on the other hand, were delicious and I was starving, but I only managed a few bites before they were gone.

Oh well, he'd offered to pay for dinner so he may as well eat it, I figured.

He excused himself to use the bathroom, and the waitress immediately came over to me. "Dave is a really special man," she whispered to me conspiratorially. "You're a lucky woman."

Suddenly I cared even less about how hungry I was.

We made the short walk to his condo in the night air that was so cold it felt like evil invisible pixies were stabbing my face in every inch of exposed flesh, but I didn't really mind that either. Then the conversation turned to birthdays. He asked me mine, and I asked him his. I told him mine is in September. He said his is in July, and I almost threw up.

I instantly changed the subject before he could confirm my gut feeling was correct. I confirmed it when I got home and scanned his Facebook page more thoroughly: He has the same birthday as Lou.

Not only is July 20th Lou's birthday, but it's also our son Sean's birthday, and Lou's dad's birthday. So it is a very significant day for us. What the hell? I thought. There are 364 other days he could have been born on. What sort of sick twist was this?

The committee thought it was a sign.

It took me a while, but eventually I agreed with them.

It was an easy move for me to shut down all communication with the other Matchelors soon after I met Dave. I wasn't shopping for those matching Christmas sweaters, but I wasn't shopping for anyone else either. I didn't ask him what his status was. He had a way of making me feel like whatever he was doing, he was doing with pure intent, and that was enough for me.

A few weeks in, I was getting stupid about things again. The more I started to feel for him, the more I tried not to. I didn't want a real relationship. I didn't want to open myself up to be hurt again. I wanted to keep my feelings under control and keep this casual.

It would only be a matter of time before he turned into a piece of shit, too, I thought. May as well expose that side of him now and get it over with.

A man who can't engage in practical jokes with me is a man who I do not want to be with. What better way to figure out if he can take a joke, I thought, than to swap out his toilet paper for fake toilet paper—the kind that looks and feels like regular toilet paper but doesn't rip?

The switch was made right before I left his place one afternoon, in a rush to get home before the kids did.

The next morning, I was reconsidering the decision.

"Dave," I texted him. "Before you are in a position to need toilet paper, there is something I should tell you."

My phone buzzed immediately. "Interesting timing," he said.

"Guess where I am right now?"

He won't admit it, but he thinks it's funny.

It didn't matter what I threw his way, not even taking him home to see my house and my kids in person was enough to drive him away.

Okay, he did drive away pretty fast. The actual experience of walking into my home, with four dogs barking at you, four boys who were a blend of fully clothed to barely clothed as per their personalities, pictures of my dead husband, and my instant transformation into mom mode was a wee bit overwhelming for him. He made a soft excuse to leave a few minutes later, and I didn't object.

Well, I thought, that was fun while it lasted. At least my kids wouldn't be upset—they'd only met him for five minutes and I told them he was a friend. It wouldn't impact them one bit, and I had been waiting for this to happen anyway, so it was all good.

But we spoke later that night, and he wasn't walking away.

In the years since, Dave has had plenty of reasons to walk away. But whatever the challenge or struggle or however being together complicates his own life, he makes it clear he is never walking away.

He's given me the gift of being a part of his kids' lives too. Being in the stepmom role is another box I never imagined I'd check in terms of life experiences, but there I go, checking away.

There is a lot about our lives together that isn't easy. It requires selflessness, humility, commitment, trust, and a never-quit mindset.

I wouldn't trade any of it.

Imagine the confidence it takes for Dave to love me, knowing he is sharing my heart. On the flip side, adjusting to his ex-wife being a part of our lives required me to develop a different kind of confidence myself. With Dave walking a tightrope between keeping the mother of his children and the woman he loves at peace with each other, we've developed a friendly relationship and work together to be the best we can for their kids.

Pretty cool, I think.

Dave brought his entrepreneurial expertise into my life too. I've never been the kind of person who enjoys the consistency of a strict routine. Knowing where I am going to be every Tuesday morning at 10 a.m., and what I will be working on, and who I will be surrounded by, and what my salary cap is, feels smothering to me. Before I met Dave, I never imagined there could be any other path for me.

I am grateful for the job I had when I met Dave. Not only did it allow me to regain my own financial stability, but it also allowed me to remember I have my own value to offer. It gave me the opportunity to apply my experience to help others, and to serve my community.

Without Dave, that would have been where my story ended, professionally. But together, we've launched our company, American Snippets, that allows me to continue to bring my gifts to the table. We've built a massive network across the country. We've impacted thousands of people, and we are growing more every month.

Loving Dave, and being loved by Dave, is a gift. But it's a gift I would never have been able to unwrap if I hadn't first learned how to love myself again. Yes, I know that sounds like a cliché. I stand by it anyway.

The day I lost my husband, I lost everything I was and believed and planned and dreamed and knew. If you had told me then that I'd be where I am now, I never would have believed you. I probably would have punched you in your stupid face.

If I had given up then, or on any day since, I would have missed all the beautiful moments I've experienced since then. My kids would have suffered more too.

The moment I decided I didn't need to find new love, love found me. The less I believed in him, the more he doubled down believing in me, until I finally believed in him too.

I don't know what tomorrow holds. That's terrifying but it's beautiful, too, isn't it?

I don't know how many days I will get to spend by Dave's side. But I do know I am surrendering to the experience of life, whatever heartbreaks it brings. I would not trade loving Lou for the pain of losing him. So I am not going to trade loving Dave for the fear of losing him either.

Life will change, and joy will come in different packages. But each day is a gift, and I am going to open it every time.

***

On my right wrist is love, and loss, and insight.
On my left hand is a new gift.
I wear both with respect and gratefulness. One complements the other.
This time I will not take it for granted.
This time, I am grateful every day.
One heart. Two loves. It is possible.
Never give up.

Author's Note

While I haven't unpacked each chapter to the same degree I do with specific keynotes or workshops or personal mentoring, I've carefully pulled enough detail from each topic to give you more than a running start at turning your own pain into purpose.

Whatever your pain point is, it will take time and dedication to learn how to flip it into a purpose. But just like any disciplined skill, once you learn it, practice, and commit to it, it becomes a natural reflex. Muscle memory applies to mindset just like it does to anything physical.

Applying even one lesson from this book will create a shift in your trajectory.

Be gracious with your grief, but not meek with it.

Be accepting of pain, but intolerant of suffering.

Be eager for progress, but not impatient.

Be persistent, but not stubborn.

All of these are key differentiators in resilience.

I love that I found the path to turn my pain into a powerful purpose. My love of our country, flawed as it is, combined with the extraordinary inspiration from our network, Dave's entrepreneurial knowledge, and lessons we've both learned, helped us determine our path is to help people strengthen themselves, their families, and their communities—all of which will lead to strengthening our country that my husband and so many others gave their lives in service of, and for which we will always bear the weight.

Dave and I make no apologies for our patriotism or our political views, but we understand that patriotism is not just about wanting people we agree with, or even like, to thrive and find fulfillment—it's about wanting that for all Americans, regardless of whether someone likes us or not. We would be thrilled to have you join us in our Great American Syndicate so we can have conversations that need to be had, support you in your path, welcome your support of others, and heal our country's heart the way we are healing our own.

It took me ten years of unnecessary suffering to reach the point that I decided the pain of healing was preferable to the pain of not healing. I hope it doesn't take that long for you. I hope you found something in this book that leads to you snapping out of stagnancy, or halting your harmful spinning, and reversing the power of your pain until you own it, instead of it owning you.

I wish I could share every single lesson I've learned on resiliency, grief, trauma, tragedy, relationships, courage, patriotism, and more—but we can't pack every favorite outfit on every trip, can we?

I'd love to stay connected with you, answer your questions, learn your story, and connect you with the amazing people in our community. This book is a great beginning to the beautiful relationship you can build with yourself and others. I am so honored to be a part of your path.

Made in the USA
Middletown, DE
04 September 2021